The business of agricultural business services

Working with smallholders in Africa

Mariana Wongtschowski, John Belt,
Willem Heemskerk and David Kahan

Editors

Royal Tropical Institute

This publication is jointly produced by:

Royal Tropical Institute (KIT)
PO Box 95001, 1090 HA, Amsterdam, Netherlands
development@kit.nl, www.kit.nl

Food and Agriculture Organization of the United Nations (FAO)
Viale delle Terme di Caracalla, 00153 Rome, Italy
www.fao.org

Agri-ProFocus
PO Box 108, 6800 AC Arnhem, Netherlands
info@agri-profocus.nl, www.agri-profocus.nl

Coordination: Mariana Wongtschowski, John Belt and Willem Heemskerk, KIT; David Kahan, FAO

Language editing: Paul Mundy, www.mamud.com

Printing: High Trade BV, Zwolle, The Netherlands

Cover photo: Loading coffee in Kenya. © Kate Holt / eyevine, www.eyevine.com

ISBN: 978 94 6022 2368

Order from: KIT Publishers, www.kitpublishers.nl

Free for download at www.kitpublishers.nl or www.fao.org/ag/ags/index/en/

Correct citation: Wongtschowski, M., J. Belt, W. Heemskerk, and D. Kahan (eds). 2013. The business of agricultural business services: Working with smallholders in Africa. Royal Tropical Institute, Amsterdam; Food and Agriculture Organization of the United Nations, Rome; and Agri-ProFocus, Arnhem.

Contents

Preface vii
Acknowledgements ix
Contributors x

1   Business services for smallholders in Africa 1

2   Historical context 9

3   Business models for business services 17

4   Cluster A: Free services 33
   Building competitiveness: Miruku in Mozambique 35
   Balancing the interests of donors and clients: 3C in Zambia 43
   Enterprise grants in Uganda: The District Livelihoods Support Programme 49
   Moving from a development to a business approach: UGAMA CSC, Rwanda 57
   Potatoes in Western Uganda: Excel Hort Consult Ltd 65

5   Cluster B: Subsidized services 73
   Farmer training centres and the IPMS programme in Ethiopia 75
   Business service centres for cocoa in Ghana 85
   Farmers in the driving seat: Imbaraga, Rwanda 93

6   Cluster C: Fully paid services 101
   The challenges of young entrepreneurs in Mozambique: Bindzu 103
   The Cassava+ project in Mozambique: DADTCO 111
   Serving beekeepers in Uganda: ESDC 119
   From urban business consulting to rural business services: Target, Ethiopia 127

7   Analysis 135

8   Towards a needs-driven model 157

   References 171
   Contributors' profiles 175

Figures

1   From a simplistic approach focused on production...11
2   ...to a more holistic approach also looking at other enabling and constrain-
    ing factors...12
3   Supply-driven model 14
4   Market-driven model..15

5   Generic business model for a service provider 23
6   Cluster A: Free business services for farmers 25
7   Alternative ways of organizing business model A1: Government or donor
    pays for services to farmers 25
8   Business model A2: Input supplier or buyer contracts service provider 26
9   Business model A3: Vouchers for services...26
10 Cluster B: In subsidized services, farmers pay a part of the cost............................27
11 Business model B1: Part-payment by farmers 27
12 Business model B2: Subsidized cooperative services for members.........................28
13 Cluster C: Farmers pay the full cost of some services 28
14 Business model C1: Services paid by the client 29
15 Business model C2: Embedded services...29

16 Miruku provides a wide range of services to its clients 36
17 Share of business models in Miruku's revenue..38
18 Miruku's business model A1 for its work with AGRA and the Muecate Union 39
19 Miruku's business model A2 for its work on the ProSavanna master plan.............40

20 Share of business models in 3C's revenue...45
21 3C's business model A1..45
22 3C's service delivery to farmers depends on suitable government policies..............48

23 DLSP's business model A1...51
24 DLSP's business model B1...52
25 Share of business models in DLSP's enterprise grants programme.........................52
26 DLSP uses the Gender Action Learning System methodology to emphasize
    gender justice and ownership..54

27 As farmers' groups grow, their needs for business services change........................59
28 UGAMA's business model A1..61
29 UGAMA's business models C1 (top) and A3 (bottom) 61
30 Share of business models in UGAMA CSC's revenue 62

31 Excel Hort's business model A1 68
32 Excel Hort's business model C1 69

33   Share of business models in Excel Hort's revenue 69

34   Market information boards display prices, news and announcements 70

35   The farmer training centres provide information on new farming techniques, improved seed and training on business management 76

36   Actors involved in service delivery in villages 77

37   Share of business models in the farmer training centres' revenue 79

38   The farmer training centres' business model B1 79

39   The business service centres' business model B1 87

40   The business service centres' business model A1 88

41   The business service centres' business model C2 89

42   Share of business models in the business service centres' revenue 89

43   Imbaraga lobbies various arms of the government to promote the interests of farmers 95

44   Imbaraga's business model B2 96

45   Imbaraga's business model A1 97

46   Share of business models in Imbaraga Northern Province's revenue 98

47   Share of business models in Bindzu's revenue 106

48   Bindzu's business model C2 106

49   How DADTCO turns cassava into beer 113

50   Share of business models in DADTCO's revenue 114

51   DADTCO's business model C2 115

52   DADTCO's current business model A1 115

53   KABECOS uses a farmer-to-farmer training scheme 120

54   Simplified outline of how ESDC and KABECOS operate 122

55   ESDC's business model C1 123

56   Share of business models in ESDC's revenue 124

57   Target's business model C1 130

58   Target's business model A1 130

59   Target's business model A3 131

60   Target's business model B1 132

61   Share of business models in Target's revenue 133

62   Proportion of different business models for different providers, based on estimated business service revenue in 2012 138

63   Private service providers maintain their financial sustainability by following multiple business models and having several sources of income 139

64   Downward accountability means that the clients (farmers) have some control over the business services 147

65   Inclusiveness means serving all types of farmers, including the poor, the disadvantaged, and women 149

66   If the playing field is uneven, private service providers can be left on the sidelines 165

Tables

1   Nine business-model building blocks...22
2   Overview of business models identified in the cases.............................24
3   Clusters of cases in this book..30
4   Characteristics of the supply-, market- and needs-driven models 159

Boxes

1   Pluralistic extension systems 3
2   Types of business services..4
3   Business development jargon 5
4   What is a business model? 21
5   Policy changes in Zambia encouraging the growth of private-sector business
     development services 47
6   DLSP in Bugiri 51
7   Idohwe group members profit from a maize mill 53
8   Atsibi *woreda*, Tigray: A sustainable farmer training centre 81
9   Apples in Chencha 129
10   Dida Cooperative Union 131
11   Key lessons and arguments from the cases: Sustainability....................145
12   Key lessons and arguments: Accountability.....................................149
13   Women can become entrepreneurs 151
14   Key lessons and arguments: Inclusiveness 153
15   Key lessons and arguments: Capacity development............................156
16   The African Union's Framework for Africa's Agricultural Productivity 164

Preface

Market liberalization, globalization, rapid urbanization, rising incomes and changing diets... they are all changing agriculture at an unprecedented speed and in diverse ways. They are creating new markets, stimulating demand for high-value products, and making it possible for farmers to produce food and other products for the market. These developments offer opportunities for farmers, but they also produce challenges and risks.

The majority of farmers – particularly smallholders – need to expand their understanding of markets and economic opportunities if they are to achieve success in running their farms as sustainable and profitable businesses. To create a viable livelihood from farming, they need to move from a sole focus on production for home consumption and occasional marketing of surpluses to producing also for the market, responding to the continuously changing market demands.

Even though farmers are innovative and entrepreneurial, they often lack the know-how to do so alone. They need advice from others; they need services.

Traditionally, farmers were served by public extensionists. In response to the trends described here and the challenge to link farmers to markets, several countries have been reconsidering extension delivery, encouraging a more pluralistic, business-oriented and demand-driven approach to providing advice to its farmers.

Governments and international donors have long tried to promote small and medium enterprises in urban areas by providing "business development services". From the mid-1990s onwards, they began adapting this approach to rural settings. Agricultural business development services – the subject of this book – include technical advice on production and postharvest handling, marketing ideas, assistance with business planning and access to credit, advice on how to organize farmers, training, links with suppliers and buyers, market information and research, etc. Such services can also be provided to other value chain actors such as local traders, input dealers and agro-processors. Some of the same services were provided by extensionists earlier on, but with a keen eye on the market. Sustainable financing of these services remains a challenge because resource-poor farmers cannot afford to pay for them.

Business service providers now operate in a pluralistic system where governmental, non-governmental, for-profit companies and farmers' organizations all play a role in service provision. They often compete with each other, and depend on subsidies from governments and donors. In this landscape and from a perspective of financial viability, new and innovative ways of ensuring broad-based coverage and financing of services need to be introduced.

It is for these reasons that this book was conceived. As a collaborative endeavour between FAO, KIT and Agri-ProFocus, it sheds new light on agricultural business development services in Africa. The objective of this book is to learn from field experiences to gain an understanding of what has worked where and why. It analyses the challenges faced by those trying to make business service provision a business in itself.

The book describes 12 cases from countries in sub-Saharan Africa. Though these cases are far from exhaustive, they nevertheless reflect a wealth of recent experience. The book identifies different ways that the public and private sectors have been working together and the gaps that must still be bridged.

Practitioners working in value chain and enterprise development, development partners who finance projects and policymakers will find this book useful for orienting their support to the agricultural sector.

We hope that this is just the beginning of a process to collect more evidence on the topic of agricultural business services from other regions of the world as a basis for cross-regional learning and sharing. Professional, accessible services are key to developing agricultural value chains that provide income to so many people, and safe food to consumers. We hope you will find the book useful and that it helps you in your endeavours.

Florence Tartanac, Group Leader – Market Linkages and Value Chains, FAO

Bart de Steenhuijsen Piters, Director, Development Policy and Practice, KIT

Hedwig Bruggeman, Director, Agri-ProFocus

Acknowledgements

We have a book! But it was not as easy as we thought… We came together in October 2012 in Addis Ababa for the writeshop that gave origin to this book. We had it all planned. But, surprisingly, the cases did not fit the boxes we had assigned to them. They were more complex, more real. We improvised, twisted and turned, looked at the cases from other perspectives. A learning process that we hope is clearly mirrored in this publication.

This book would not have been possible without the hard work and commitment of many people, all of whom twisted and turned with us. To begin with, the "case owners" who attended the writeshop in Addis: without their openness and honesty, we would have had a very different book! Rik Delnoye worked with us in the early stages in selecting the cases and coaching the case authors. We thank Rik for starting this process with such dedication. Wouter Kleijn and Kati Oudendijk collected and analysed data on several cases in Mozambique and Uganda, respectively, as part of their MSc studies. We hope their work (and experience) was of as much help for them as it was for us.

Paul Mundy, our editor, has been of fundamental importance in transforming our draft thoughts into full text. Yitagesu Mergia has drawn the wonderful line drawings that explain and illustrate the text. Harun Samu provided efficient and informed logistics support. Thanks to Dirk Hoekstra of the International Livestock Research Institute for his hospitality and support.

We counted on a number of peer reviewers for this book: Peter Gildemacher at the Royal Tropical Institute, and Christel Schiphorst and Wim Goris of Agri-ProFocus in Arnhem, the Netherlands. Our thanks for their constructive and very helpful feedback and critique.

Wim Goris and Christel Schiphorst also played an important role in bringing those cases together. The Food and Agriculture Organization of the United Nations and Agri-ProFocus have also financially contributed to the production of this book.

Finally, we would like to thank the Dutch Directorate for International Cooperation (DGIS) for their support in the form of core funding to KIT.

Mariana Wongtschowski, John Belt, Willem Heemskerk, David Kahan

Editors

Contributors

Full contact details and brief biographies of the contributors appear at the end of the book.

Case authors

Ethiopia

Nigatu Alemayu
Improving Productivity and Market Success of Ethiopian Farmers (IPMS)

Getnet Haile
Target Business Consultants plc

Ghana

Prince Dodoo
Agribusiness Systems International (ASI)

Mozambique

Chissungue Haje António
Miruku

Márcia Maposse
Bindzu

Isabel Mazive
Dutch Agricultural Development & Trading Company (DADTCO)

Rwanda

Joseph Gafaranga
Imbaraga

J. Richard N. Kanyarukiga
Higher Institute of Agriculture & Animal Production (ISAE)

Innocent Simpunga
UGAMA CSC

Uganda

Ambrose Bugaari
Effective Skills Development Consultants (ESDC)

Adeline Rwashana Muheebwa
District Livelihoods Support Programme (DLSP)

May Lesley Murungi
Excel Hort Consult Ltd

Zambia

Catherine Phiri
3C Development Management & Entrepreneurship Experts Ltd

Writeshop and production

Coordination and editing
John Belt, Willem Heemskerk, Mariana Wongtschowski
Royal Tropical Institute (KIT)

David Kahan
Food and Agriculture Organization of the United Nations (FAO)

Resource persons
Wim Goris
Agri-ProFocus

Gerrit Holtland
Agri-ProFocus Agri-Hub Ethiopia

Editing and layout
Paul Mundy

Artist
Yitagesu Mergia

Logistics
Harun Thomas Samu
Facilitating Farmers' Access to Remunerative Markets (FFARM plc)

The business of agricultural business services

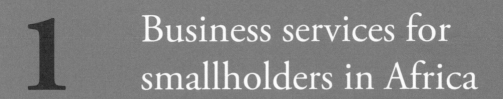

1
Business services for smallholders in Africa

Entrepreneurship training, Ghana
Photo: ASI, Ghana

1   Business services for smallholders in Africa

Worldwide the demand for food is growing, particularly in the developing world. Hunger is still widespread, often as a result of unequal income distribution. While Africa is the continent with the biggest challenges, many also regard it as having the largest potential to deal with them.

Agriculture in Africa has seen some fundamental changes during the last decades. It has become more dynamic. State involvement in food markets has declined, giving way to the market as the mechanism to coordinate supply and demand. That has left farmers without a guaranteed buyer, and in doubt about the price they will receive.

A change in thinking and policy about the role of the public sector in agricultural extension led to reductions in public spending on it. As a result, many extension services, once purely government-run, have been partly or wholly privatized. New operators from the private sector have arisen to complement the shrinking government services and take advantage of the new opportunities in the sector. But this has happened only to a limited extent and certainly not everywhere, typically not in remote areas with cash-strapped farmers and consumers.

Larger-scale farmers have been able to cope better with these changes than smallholders. They have the volume of output they need to attract buyers who are willing to pay more for bulk deliveries. They have the capital they need to invest in improved production, processing and storage facilities. And they have the money to pay for business services.

Many smallholders remain without some or all the services they need to market their output profitably. And agriculture in Africa is typically about smallholder farming: market-oriented producers, subsistence farmers, and those in between. Smallholders are key to raising food output and increasing the flow of food to consumers. As most smallholders are poor, increased production and improved marketing are also vital to food security and local development.

The need for this book

To rise to the challenges described above, smallholders need to work the logic of markets. For that they need skills – and they do not come spontaneously. To make farming a

National and international efforts to revitalize extension services – also referred to as 'advisory services' – "have resulted in a variety of institutional reforms: decentralization, contracting/outsourcing, public-private partnerships, and privatization have started to transform conventional models of public-sector agricultural advisory services. Revitalizing the public-sector services has also been an important reform strategy.

"In addition, new actors have entered the scene to provide and finance advisory services, including non-governmental organizations (NGOs), farmer groups and community-based organizations. Private-sector companies provide embedded advisory services, which are integrated in commercial transactions such as sale of inputs or contract farming. The term 'pluralistic' has been coined to capture the emerging diversity of institutional options in providing and financing agricultural advisory services."

Source: Birner at al. 2009

business, farmers need specific services to help them in doing so: business services. And these services need to cater to a wide range of types of farmers. The same holds true for other value chain actors such as local traders, warehouse managers, input suppliers and local processors: they also need business services to be able to cope with the dynamic environment they find themselves in.

These services have to be provided within – still poorly understood – pluralistic extension systems, under which private, NGOs and governmental organizations provide different types of advisory services, funded by different sources (Box 1).

As an approach, the provision of business services has a long history in urban areas. For example, governments and development agencies have provided incentives for small businesses, offered potential entrepreneurs training and advice, set up business incubators, sponsored courses in entrepreneurship and management, etc. The challenge is to adapt such services to the rural world, and to build a strong "pluralistic system" for service delivery, regulation (quality control) and funding of such services.

This book sheds light to one facet of such a pluralistic system. It looks at business service providers in particular, and discusses a number of issues. What type of farmers do they cater to? How do they survive as "business" on their own? What challenges do they face? Who funds them? What kind of business services do they deliver?

And further: what are the roles of governments and donors in supporting an extension system that allows private, non-profit and public service providers to play the role they are best fit to play?

Answering these questions, in turn, will contribute to a better understanding of how a pluralistic service system that is responsive to farmers' needs may work in practice. We deem this useful to policymakers, donors and business development service providers alike: the same actors who have been experimenting with putting such a system into practice.

Defining business development services

Farmers and other local actors rely on two broad categories of services to make farming a business:

- **Provision of tangible goods**, like money to invest, seed, fertilizer, transport, storage facilities, equipment, etc.

- **Business services**, such as technical advice, contacts and information.

A range of specialist private companies generally supply the **tangible items**. Banks and microfinance organizations offer credit, along with various other financial services such as savings, payment and insurance. Input suppliers sell fertilizer, seed and pesticides. Equipment dealers sell tools and machinery. Transporters pick up produce and haul it to its destination. Storage companies dry grain and keep it in silos and warehouses. Millers grind grain into flour. Sometimes such services are subsidized by governments and external donors. Where this is not the case, farmers are commonly prepared to pay for at least part of the cost.

In contrast, **business services** are "software" rather than hardware: they involve knowledge and skills rather than objects you can hold. They embrace the non-tangible, non-storable items provided to farmers in order to increase, directly or indirectly, the productivity of their resources.

Box 2 lists some types of business services that are provided by the organizations described in Chapters 4–6 in this book. There is a huge diversity here, and this diversity is important: it illustrates the many different types of services that farmers need. These services are

> **Box 3   Business development jargon**
>
> The field of business services has led to a wealth of abbreviations. Here are some of the more common ones.
> - **ABDS**   Agricultural business development services
> - **BDS**   Business development services
> - **MOAAS**   Market-oriented agricultural advisory services
> - **RBDS**   Rural business development services

provided through a range of methods: training, coaching, demonstrations, meetings, discussions, coordination, facilitation, documents, announcements, etc.

Some business services are closely tied to particular tangible items: a new machine or a container of pesticide may be useless without instructions on how to use it. Advice to grow a particular crop variety is of little value if the seed of that variety are nowhere to be found. Other business services are less tied to particular items: creating a record-keeping system and forming a marketing group are examples.

Different names, one main concept

A number of approaches have emerged to provide farmers and other actors with business services (see Chapter 2). These are referred to by different names: rural business development services, agricultural business development services, market oriented agricultural advisory services and value-chain-development advisory services (Box 3). For simplicity's sake, and to avoid semantic discussions, we refer to them all simply as "business services".

How this book was produced

This book is the result of collaboration between the Royal Tropical Institute (KIT, a centre of knowledge and expertise in international development), Agri-ProFocus (a Netherlands-based network working on farmer entrepreneurship), and the Food and Agriculture Organization of the United Nations (FAO). The production team was coordinated by KIT. The book was drafted through a writeshop, an intensive, participatory workshop to produce information materials that follows a process originally developed by the International Institute of Rural Reconstruction (Mundy et al. 2006).

The 12 cases in this book were identified through the Agri-ProFocus network and through other professional networks and contacts. The writeshop was held in Addis Ababa on 8–12 October 2012. The writeshop included introductions to the concept and history of business services (these form the basis of Chapter 2), and brief presentations by the authors of each case. Small groups of participants identified the business models followed by each service provider. They discussed the sustainability, accountability and inclusiveness of the services and of the providers themselves, and developed recommendations for governments and donors about business services. The results of these discussions are included in the chapters on business models (Chapter 3) and analysis and recommendations (Chapters 7 and 8).

At the same time, each author in turn met with a resource person and the editor to clarify aspects of their case and to rewrite the descriptions in light of the group discussions. They also selected photographs to illustrate each case, and conceptualized the artwork, which the artist turned into the line drawings. This process of rewriting and illustration resulted in the text of Chapters 4–6.

After the writeshop, the production team remained in Addis Ababa for a further week to refine the drafts and produce a semi-final manuscript, which the editors turned into the book you are now reading.

Audience

The authors of the cases are managers and staff of business service providers. They wrote the original manuscripts describing their organizations, and contributed to the discussions that resulted in the introductory and analysis chapters. Other practitioners, in private companies, donor-funded projects, NGOs and government programmes, will find much to learn from their experiences.

This book will also interest policymakers in national and local governments, as well as donors and development agencies, who design policies and decide how to support market-driven agricultural development.

What is in this book

This book is about business service providers, and their work with smallholders and small and medium enterprises. It draws on 12 cases from six African countries: Ethiopia, Ghana, Mozambique, Rwanda, Uganda and Zambia. These cover a range of services. Some services are free, some subsidized, and some where the client pays the full cost. Most of the service providers are private companies, though some are NGOs, public-sector organizations or farmers' organizations. They all provide a range of business services to farmers and other rural clients. They both supply their clients with straight services (such as providing market information), and aim to build the clients' capacity (such as training them on marketing).

The book is organized as follows:

Chapter 2 explores different trends that contributed to a revival of the concept of **business services** and looks at the different models used to put the concept into practice.

Chapter 3 introduces the various **business models** that service providers use when bringing services to their clients. We have identified seven different business models, and clustered them into three categories: free, subsidized and fully paid.

Each of the next four chapters presents several cases that illustrate these models. Each case describes a single service provider, and deals either with its activities in general, or focuses on a particular project that it is engaged in.

Chapter 4, on **free services**, presents five cases where services are provided to farmers for free, paid for by international donors or national governments:

- **Miruku**, a company that trains NGOs, government and private companies in Mozambique in governance, business management and marketing

- **3C**, a private company in Zambia that builds the capacity of local NGOs and farmers' groups.

- The **District Livelihoods Support Programme**, a government project in Uganda that offers enterprise grants to farmers' groups.

- **UGAMA CSC**, an NGO that serves farmers' groups and cooperatives in Rwanda.

- **Excel Hort**, a company that provides consultancy services to cooperatives and agricultural entrepreneurs.

Chapter 5, on **subsidized services**, has three cases where farmers pay part of the costs of the services they receive:

- **Farmer training centres** supported by the Improving Productivity and Market Success of Ethiopian Farmers (IPMS) project in Ethiopia, which involves collaboration between the public-sector extension system and international research organizations.

- **Business service centres** which offer a range of services to cocoa farmers in Ghana, supported by ASI.

- **Imbaraga**, a farmer organization in Rwanda that provides a range of services to its members.

Chapter 6 turns to **fully paid services** – where farmers and other clients pay for the services they get. This chapter presents four cases. In the first two, both from Mozambique, the services are embedded as part of another transaction:

- **Bindzu**, a company that provides advice and other services along with agricultural inputs that farmers buy.

- **DADTCO**, a cassava-processing company that organizes and trains farmers and buys cassava from them.

In two more cases, from Uganda and Ethiopia, the farmers and their organizations pay for the services as a separate transaction:

- **Effective Skills Development Consultants (ESDC)**, a company that supports enterprise development in agribusiness and nature conservation.

- **Target**, a consultancy company in Ethiopia that advises NGOs, businesses, the government, international organizations and cooperatives.

Chapter 7, Analysis, brings together the main lessons from these cases. It focuses on four areas: the **financial sustainability** of the service provider and service provision, the **accountability** of the service provider to the client, the level of **inclusiveness** of the services, and the **capacity needs** of service providers.

Chapter 8, Towards a needs-driven model, presents a number of conclusions of what a next generation of business service providers could look like and operate. It elaborates on the policy needs to support such a new generation of service providers and provision.

At the end of the book we provide a list of references and contact information for the contributors.

2 Historical context

Training for farmers on business skills
Photo: Harun Thomas, FFARM, Ethiopia

2   Historical context

The changes in agriculture and extension systems, outlined in the previous chapter, have led to a need for a shift in how services are provided in rural areas. Experiences from the urban sector have provided inspiration for this shift. The rural version of business services is the result of a number of developments. These are discussed in the first part of this chapter.

Since they were first put in practice as a donor approach in the mid-1990s, business services have undergone a number of important changes. These are discussed in the second part of this chapter.

Different trends come together

The importance of the market

Rapid changes in market environment for agriculture are affecting smallholder farmers everywhere. Some of the changes include (World Bank 2007):

- Markets, not production, increasingly drive agricultural development.

- The production, trade and consumption environment for agricultural products is becoming more dynamic and evolving in unpredictable ways (e.g., due to rising energy costs, the push towards biofuels, and climate change).

- Knowledge, information and technologies are increasingly being generated and diffused by the private sector.

- Information and communication technologies have transformed the capacity of farmers, especially large-scale, commercial producers, to take advantage of new technologies developed elsewhere.

- Agricultural development is increasingly taking place in a globalized setting.

These developments pose extraordinary challenges for rural producers, but may also offer them great opportunities. Most need to expand their understanding of markets and economic opportunities if they are to achieve more market success.

Figure 1   From a simplistic approach focused on production…

From a focus on production to looking at markets

Practitioners started to consider how extension services could help farmers to take advantage of these opportunities and deal with the new organizational and financing challenges facing them. This meant advisory services should help farmers to move beyond subsistence to become a motor of local development.

The concept of "market oriented agricultural advisory services" (another name for business services, as discussed in Chapter 1) was then recognized as a mainstream strategy for smallholder commercialization (Chipeta et al. 2008). This calls for a shift in the types of services provided to farmers. Instead of a focus on increasing productivity, service providers should cover a range of different areas, including production, farm management, postharvest handling, credit access, and marketing.

Innovation comes from interaction

Practitioners and researchers alike argue that innovation is a product of the interaction, joint work and collaboration of a large number of actors (Spielman et al. 2009). But widely used extension models – still used in several parts of the world – treated innovation as a set of one-size-fits-all technologies, to be provided by a monopolistic public sector. New thinking calls for advisory services that recognize the importance of different actors (public sector, private companies along the value chains, service providers, farmers) in providing customized advice with pluralistic delivery channels (Christoplos 2010, Davis et al. 2012).

Figure 2 **...to a more holistic approach also looking at other enabling and constraining factors**

Re-emergence of public investment in advisory services

Before the 1990s, extension services were seen as a service to be provided solely by governments. During the 1990s, however, confidence declined in the effectiveness of public-sector extension agencies. That led to the emergence of an alternative paradigm, where it was assumed that market-based solutions and the privatization of extension provision could become an effective and sustainable base for development. Many governments and aid agencies experimented with this. Services for relatively well-off commercial farmers were (and still are) increasingly dominated by private advisory service providers, but these rarely served the rural poor. In many countries, privatization (often achieved merely by withdrawing funding for public-sector agencies) resulted in most farmers losing access altogether to impartial, independent advice. This showed the need for wider reform of extension system: one that promotes pluralism while recognizing the need for public financial support (Christoplos 2010, Davis and Heemskerk 2012, Swanson et al. 2010).

Learning from the support to small and medium enterprises

The required set of services for agriculture could draw inspiration from the history of business development services to small and medium enterprises in urban areas. In the early

1990s, NGO initiatives such as the Grameen Bank in Bangladesh had shown microcredit as a promising way to bring the rural poor into market-led economic development. The idea was that a small loan, to be repaid at the market interest rate, together with hard work and reinforced by social pressure, are enough for rural people to get themselves out of poverty. But over time, donors, multilateral organizations, NGOs and grassroots organizations realized that for many rural households, microcredit was not enough: they did not have the knowledge and skills they needed to earn a living from their own small businesses. Non-financial enterprise development services were needed to give them these skills.

That led to the provision of business services as an approach, at first to complement the provision of credit with the management and marketing assistance needed for small enterprises to be profitable. This approach grew out of donors' conviction that providing such assistance was primarily the responsibility of private-sector actors.

The approach was originally conceived to develop small and medium enterprises especially in and around cities and towns. There is little information on how well the approach has worked among smallholder farmers in rural areas. Research has largely been done in urban areas, or at small- and medium rural enterprises – and not with farmers.

Business services gained international momentum – and became more commonly applied to rural areas – between the mid-1990s and the mid-2000s. They have waned in popularity since. In the early 2000s, the once-vibrant business development services working group of the Committee of Donor Agencies for Small Enterprise Development ceased its yearly revisions of the "BDS blue book" – the guiding principles for donor interventions in this area.

In the agricultural sector, support for business development services was superseded as an approach by value chain development and "making markets work for the poor". Those programmes that remain combine value-chain or sector-specific programming with the development of service markets to improve the competitiveness of selected value chains.

Recently among value-chain practitioners, awareness has grown that value chains do not operate in a vacuum, and that market forces alone cannot ensure that smallholders are included in a particular chain. Once more, services to smallholders are considered essential.

Models of implementation

Important shifts have taken place in the way the development of business development services has been supported by donors, both in urban and rural settings, over the last decades. We take stock of these shifts by describing two main models of donor support: supply-driven and market-driven (Kahan 2007, 2011). We do so to understand how the cases in this book fit into the different paradigms these models represent.

The **supply-driven** approach was dominant until the mid-1990s. In this, services were designed according to the agenda of the delivering agency or the funder (development agencies). This was also referred to as the provider-centric model. Donor agencies provided funding to set up or strengthen service suppliers, both NGOs and private companies. The

Tools
Capacity-strengthening inputs
Skills training
Product development
Seed capital and institutional development subsidies

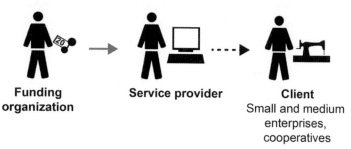

| **Funding organization** | **Service provider** | **Client** Small and medium enterprises, cooperatives |

Figure 3   Supply-driven model

provider in turn supplied services to clients (Figure 3). The services identified depended largely on what the supplier thought was needed. This model was implemented mostly in urban areas.

The predominately supply-side orientation of this approach produced distorting effects. Service providers became dependent on subsidies, and they tended to regard themselves as being responsible to the donor, not the client. As a result, the services provided did not meet clients' demands. Many services ended up being too expensive and ultimately unsustainable. Moreover, this approach prevented commercial services from developing, as they were unable to compete against the subsidized providers.

While it ensured a broad coverage among target clients, the model failed to address some fundamental questions, including:

- How can business services be made more affordable (potentially reaching the rural areas) and genuinely address the needs of clients?

- What can be done to ensure quality in service delivery, as well as outreach?

This model is still being used in many places – as shown by some of the cases in this book. These questions remain therefore pertinent.

The **demand- or market-driven model** (Figure 4) emerged in the mid-1990s. It reflected a worry, at the time, about sustainability and client-orientation of services. The model was based on the principle that the client pays. The goal was to create, develop and enable the evolution of a well-functioning market for service provision. Under this approach the funding organization acted as a facilitator, providing support to both the service providers and the target clients. Tools such as vouchers, market information and market-awareness campaigns were used to generate market demand for the services.

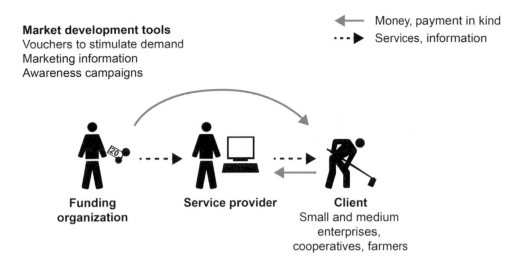

Market development tools
Vouchers to stimulate demand
Marketing information
Awareness campaigns

←———— Money, payment in kind
---▶ Services, information

Funding organization

Service provider

Client
Small and medium enterprises, cooperatives, farmers

Figure 4   Market-driven model

As with any new paradigm, there are purists and gradualists. Some felt that to develop very weak markets that serve the poor, it is necessary to subsidize direct service delivery for a time, phasing it out as the market develops. Some market development activities that temporarily subsidize service delivery include:

- Matching grants and vouchers that farmers can use to buy services.

- Contracts for service providers to serve small enterprises.

- Operating or "deficit" financing to help service providers get started, through investments that are actually never paid back to the donor.

- Services to test and develop new business models.

- Playing a role in a sub-sector, for example as a wholesaler, to demonstrate that the output market is viable.

Supporters of these types of subsidies point out that the short-term nature of many business service initiatives also pushed them toward providing services directly in order to have an impact quickly.

Opponents are sceptical about the "weaning" process, and doubt the effectiveness of development organizations that establish profitable private enterprises. Instead, they recommend finding private-sector solutions right from the start of a project, providing only training and technical assistance to suppliers, and temporarily stimulating demand through information and linking services to small enterprises. Even weak markets, they argue, are best developed by supporting local initiatives.

In addition, the sceptics say that the approach puts insufficient emphasis on the weak institutional and market situations in many developing countries, and on the difficulty of providing services to the huge number of enterprises, many of them tiny, that are not in a position to access commercial service providers. Proponents believe that with some facilitation, service providers will cater to small enterprises, and that those enterprises will purchase services that increase their own profitability. Instead, the most capable service providers typically cater to large and multinational companies. They have little interest in assisting small enterprises.

Where do we stand now?

While writing the book, we reflected about how the service providers described in the following chapters fit (if at all) these models. We also wanted to understand how they responded to the many changes the agricultural sector has seen since the 1990s, when the market development model was clearly in fashion.

What we found is that in practice, business service initiatives are much messier. These different models co-exist, and to a certain extent, adapt to local realities. The models as such still stand: either the focus is on providing support, or on stimulating demand, based on a clear belief that the market will take care of any issues related to sustainability of service provision and provider.

Important questions remain: how to ensure service providers can survive after donor support ends? What is the role of public service provision? How to ensure that services respond to farmers' needs, even where farmers cannot pay for them? These are some of the questions we will discuss in this book.

In the final chapters we will argue that a system where the supply-driven and market-driven models co-exist is not adequate to respond to rural realities. Though service providers are thriving, they still work in a project mode, time-bound and with relatively few farmers. A more dramatic change is needed in the support for – and supply of – business development services. We refer to this alternative model as the "needs-driven model".

In the next chapter, we discuss the relationship between business service suppliers, clients and donors. We believe these relationships have an important role in defining the way services are provided to farmers – and provide a glimpse of the strengths and weaknesses of the models presented above.

3 Business models for business services

Stakeholder meeting and project planning at the FAO field office in Kabale
Photo: FAO, Uganda

3   Business models for business services

This chapter outlines the interactions among the different actors who are involved in business development services. It starts by defining who these actors are, focusing especially on the service providers. It then discusses how they provide services to which clients, and where they get funding to pay for this.

Actors

Business services involve three main types of actors: clients, service providers, and funders.

- **Clients** are the people or organizations that receive the services. They may be farmers, informal or formal groups, micro and small enterprises, and community-based organizations. In this book, the clients are farmers or their organizations, unless otherwise indicated.

- **Service providers** are the individuals or organizations that deliver the business services to the clients. They may be private companies, public-sector organizations such as branches of national or local governments, NGOs, or farmers' organizations. **Back-up services providers** (van Weperen 2011) are service providers that train, coach or provide any other service to other service providers.

- **Funders** are the individuals or organizations that pay for the services. In some cases it is the clients themselves who pay for the services they receive. Often, though, it is a government programme, a development organization, donor agency, international NGO or a company further along in the value chain. They may fully or partly finance the services provided to clients, either directly to the service provider or through the clients.

Who are the service providers?

Various service providers deliver services to a range of clients. The key is to identify the best fixes: what type of supplier can best serve certain types or categories of users, or respond best to certain service needs?

The service providers fall into four main types: private sector, public sector, civil society (NGOs), and farmers' organizations. We discuss each in turn.

Private sector

In principle, private service providers have no bias towards small- or large-scale farmers. They work with any customer provided they are – directly or indirectly – paid to do so. The high transaction costs of working with large numbers of smallholders, however, often mean that the price of services is unaffordable.

Services are often "embedded" in a transaction. A wide variety of such services exist. An input supplier may sell seed, feed, chemicals or equipment, and at the same time advise farmers on how to use them. A bank or microfinance institute may offer a loan, along with advice on how to run a business. The input supplier or bank may provide the service directly, or it may contract a specialized service provider to do so. Embedded service providers tend to work with larger farmers because of the high transaction costs of working with many small farmers. In some cases, public resources are used to cover part of these transaction costs and enable such service providers to work with smallholders.

Seven of the 12 cases in this book tell the stories of private-sector service providers: **Bindzu**, **DADTCO** and **Miruku** in Mozambique, **Excel Hort** and **ESDC** in Uganda, **Target** in Ethiopia, and **3C** in Zambia.

Public sector

Public agricultural extension systems are often run by national ministries. They tend to be structured in a top-down way, and geared towards one-size-fits-all technology transfer. Attempts to bring about institutional change in this bureaucratic context have had mixed success.

Among others, we note (adapted from Anderson 2007):

- Declining numbers of extension staff in many countries due to diminishing financial resources (both at national and local levels). Fewer resources often also mean a lack of fuel or transport to get extensionists into the field.

- A shortage of competent subject-matter specialists, especially in emerging areas such as high-value crops.

- A lack of farm management and marketing skills among extension staff at all levels.

- A deficit of other professional skills, such as facilitating institutional linkages or helping farmers to organize into groups.

- Few in-service capacity-building opportunities to respond to demand for better skills and knowledge.

In some countries, extension services have been decentralized and are now the responsibility of local governments. They still retain the public delivery and funding characteristics of traditional centralized extension. The main advantage expected from decentralization is improved accountability, as agents become employees of the local government, which – if democratically elected – is eager to please its clientele-electorate. That is expected to improve the extension agents' incentives and lead to better service (Anderson 2007). Others have reacted to this by having all extension officers on performance-based contracts, as is the case in Uganda.

Two examples in this book describe the work of public-sector service providers: **DLSP** in Uganda and the **farmer training centres** in Ethiopia.

Non-government organizations

Rural-based NGOs have delivered agricultural extension and advisory services since they first appeared in the 1960s. They have done so because the poor, their primary target group, often has no means of living other than agriculture.

When public-sector extension agencies began to decline, there was a hope that local and international NGOs would help fill the resulting gap. Activities were contracted out to these organizations on a significant scale. Many NGOs have innovated and have provided greater flexibility in responding to the demands of poor farmers. But their ability to scale up successful approaches has proven limited. In addition, NGOs generally work through short-term projects, leading to problems of continuity in delivering the service.

This book has two examples of services delivered by NGOs: the **business service centres** in Ghana established by ASI, and **UGAMA** in Rwanda.

Farmers' organizations

Farmers' organizations are increasingly regarded as essential part of the institutional landscape of a healthy and balanced agricultural sector. They range from small, informal groups, farmer field and business schools, formal cooperatives, associations or unions of cooperatives, to national-level federations.

Farmers' organizations in many countries recognize that there are serious gaps in access to appropriate, impartial advice. They are beginning to identify services their members need, and to provide them to their members. This is potentially an important form of farmer-driven extension, but as yet these services are generally limited in scope. Most farmers' organizations are struggling to balance a range of demands for extension with other, often more pressing, tasks. Furthermore, these farmers' organizations are often weak, especially in terms of being representative of their members and inclusive of women as well as men smallholders. They themselves need advice to develop their organizations and their capacities to empower all their members (and potential members) in product marketing, policy formulation and setting priorities for inclusive services (Kahan 2011).

In practice, the distinction between a local NGO and a farmers' organization is not always clear cut. Farmer organizations can therefore suffer from the same flaws as NGOs, such as low continuity in service provision.

This book contains one example of a farmers' organization that provides services: **Imbaraga** in Rwanda. In addition, the case on ESDC includes a description of KABECOS, a beekeepers' cooperative in Uganda.[1]

The different ways actors come together

While the details of the relationships between clients, providers and funders vary, these interactions fall into a number of broad patterns, which we call "business models" (Box 4).

We make use of the business model concept as an analytical tool to understand how a business service provider intends to operate, interacts with its clients, coverd costs and – at times – makes profits. The results of a business model analysis allow the service provider to understand where it needs to innovate in order to compete more efficiently or to reach its desired target customers.

Osterwalder et al. (2005) define three main pillars of business models, and their respective building blocks (Table 1). Figure 5 depicts a generic business model for a service provider, drawing on the building blocks defined above. The cases in this book describe the building blocks for the service providers in general terms. Those that relate to "customer interface" are dealt with under the headings of accountability and inclusiveness. The building blocks for financial management are discussed under "financial sustainability".

When defining a typology for the service providers' business models, we have chosen to characterize them by looking mainly at the flow of resources and services between the clients, funders and service providers.

Most of the service providers described in Chapters 4–6 follow a combination of business models, depending on the service they provide. They may charge the full cost for services such as mapping or soil tests; they may charge a reduced cost for other services (such as training); and they may offer certain types of service for free (such as advice on how to use fertilizers).

---

1   More cases on farmers' organizations will be documented and analysed through the "farm–firm rela-tionships" project, a collaboration between KIT, Agri-ProFocus and the Centre for Development Innovation at Wageningen University and Research Centre.

Table 1   Nine business-model building blocks

Pillar	Business-model building block	Description
Product	Value proposition	Gives an overall view of a company's bundle of products and services
Customer interface	Target customer	Describes the segments of customers a company wants to offer value to
	Delivery channel	Describes the various means of the company to get in touch with its customers
	Relationship	Explains the kind of links a company establishes between itself and its different customer segments
Infrastructure management	Value configuration	Describes the arrangement of activities and resources
	Core competency	Outlines the competencies necessary to execute the company's business model
	Partner network	Portrays the network of cooperative agreements with other companies necessary to efficiently offer and commercialize value
Financial aspects	Cost structure	Sums up the monetary consequences of the means employed in the business model
	Revenue model	Describes the way a company makes money through a variety of revenue flows

Source: Osterwalder, Pigneur and Tucci 2005

A service provider may also apply different business models for different clients. For example, the service provider may offer a training course to a group of large, commercial farmers, and to a smallholders' cooperative. It charges the large farmers the full cost of the course, but demands only a nominal fee from the co-op. It can do this because a donor or the government subsidizes the smallholders' course.

Over time, a service may move from one model to another. For example, the service provider may start out by providing a service for free in order to test and build demand; when demand is established, it may later shift to charging the client for all or part of the cost.

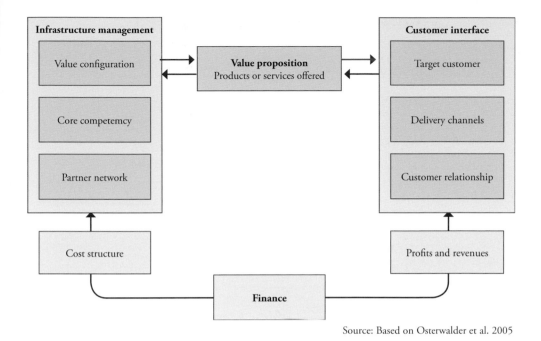

Source: Based on Osterwalder et al. 2005

Figure 5   Generic business model for a service provider

Seven business models

We have identified seven main business models from the cases presented in Chapters 4–6 and experiences elsewhere. This list does not pretend to be comprehensive: other models will exist, and differences exist within the models described here.

For analytical purposes, we have organized the seven models into three main clusters: (A) **free**, (B) **subsidized**, and (C) **fully paid** (Table 2).

In addition to these three clusters, we found that service providers also act as chain actors, doing business in the value chain. The service provider buys products from farmers and sells them to a buyer such as a processor, retailer or exporter. It may also process the product itself. Though this is not a business model for service provision, it is often an important source of revenue for service providers.

These models are a simplification of reality, as will become apparent when we look at the individual cases in Chapters 4–6. Real-life models often involve many actors: a primary farmers' group, a secondary marketing association and an umbrella farmers' union; several service providers offering different services; different sources of funding; and a strategy to shift from one model (such as free services) to another (subsidized or client-pays). Nevertheless, we believe that this simplified view gives insights into the basic approaches that the service providers use.

Table 2   Overview of business models identified in the cases

Cluster	Business model	Description	Funder	Service provider	Clients
A Free services	A1	Largely free services	Donor, government	Public or private	Farmers, small enterprises, other service providers
	A2	Paid by companies, delivered to farmers	Companies	Private	Farmers, small enterprises
	A3	Voucher	Government, donor	Private	Farmers, cooperatives
B Subsidized services	B1	Part-payment by farmers	Government, donor Fees, in-kind contributions	Private	Farmers (group)
	B2	Subsidized cooperative services for members	Government, donor Membership fees	Cooperative	Cooperative members
C Fully paid services	C1	Paid by client	Paid by client	Private	Entrepreneurs, cooperatives
	C2	Embedded services	Client: embedded in price paid for other transactions	Input or output company	Farmers

Cluster A: Free business services to farmers

This cluster looks at business models where farmers do not pay for the services they get. These are provided completely "for free", i.e., paid by someone other than the final client. In these models, the service provider may be a private company, an NGO or a government body or project. The funds may come from the government, an international donor or an NGO.

Business model A1: Government or donor pays for services to farmers

This is the most common business model, accounting for half or more of the turnover in seven of the cases in this book. The donor or government directly finances a service provider, which then delivers a service to farmers, associations or other service providers. It is a linear model and functions either in a "project mode", or as part of conventional governmental extension systems.

Figure 6   Cluster A: Free business services for farmers

In some situations, a service provider offers services to another service provider, which in turn serves the farmers. We call the first step in this chain "back-up services". These aim to build the capacity of the client service provider, for example, by training its staff how to make business plans or organize farmers. The client then uses these skills in its work with farmers.

Figure 7   Alternative ways of organizing business model A1: Government or donor pays for services to farmers

Business model A2: Input supplier or buyer contracts service provider

An agribusiness company contracts a service provider to deliver services to farmers. The company may be an input supplier or a buyer. The input supplier wants farmers to get the services so they will use the inputs correctly, and will buy inputs in the next season. The buyer wants the farmers to produce more output (or a higher quality) that it can buy.

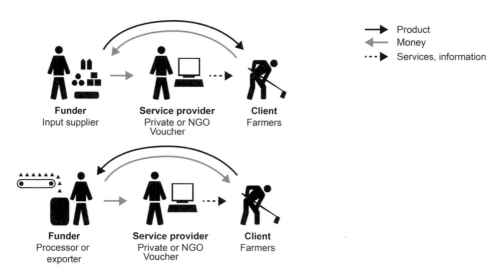

Figure 8   **Business model A2: Input supplier or buyer contracts service provider**

Business model A3: Vouchers for services

Farmers receive vouchers that they can use to buy services from a provider. The provider then redeems the vouchers with the funder in exchange for cash. The vouchers are financed by a grant from the governments or donor, or through levies imposed at a point in the value chain. In some cases the farmers can select the service provider they want to use; in other cases they can go to only one provider, but can choose which services they want. International NGOs also use this system: for instance they give a cooperative the resources to hire the services of a company; the cooperative can choose which company they want to hire.

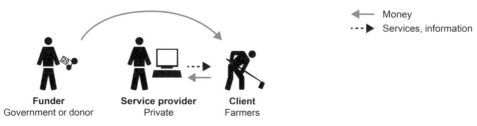

Figure 9   **Business model A3: Vouchers for services**

The business of agricultural business services

Cluster B: Subsidized business services for farmers

This cluster refers to services which are partly paid by farmers, cooperatives or other clients (in kind or cash) and partly paid by donors. There are two variations in this business model.

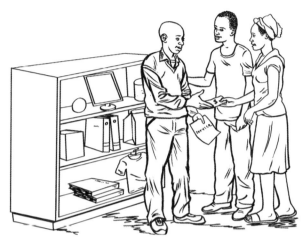

Figure 10   Cluster B: In subsidized services, farmers pay a part of the cost

Business model B1: Part-payment by farmers

Farmers pay some of the costs of the services they receive, or they contribute in kind, for example by providing labour or materials. The bulk of the cost is covered by the funder – usually the government or a donor. The fees may be paid by individual farmers or by groups.

Figure 11   Business model B1: Part-payment by farmers

Business model B2: Subsidized cooperative services for members

The cooperative provides services to its members, either directly or to a group of trainers, who then deliver the services to local groups or individuals. Services are supported by a high level of voluntarism in the cooperative and through membership fees, allied with external funding from the government or a donor.

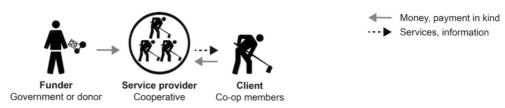

Figure 12   Business model B2: Subsidized cooperative services for members

Cluster C: Fully paid services

In this cluster, the client pays the full cost of the services. The client may pay for the service directly (as when a farmer pays the full cost of attending a training course). Or he or she may pay indirectly, for example, for advice when buying inputs, or for services when selling produce. We refer to such indirect payments as **embedded services**.

Figure 13   Cluster C: Farmers pay the full cost of some services

Business model C1: Services paid by the client

This is the simplest of all the models: the clients get a service, and pay the full cost of it. Such clients are often those that have a certain scale: big commercial farmers, or cooperatives of small farmers. Cooperatives may also provide services to their members in return for a fee.

Service provider
Public, private
or cooperative

Client
Farmers

← Money
···▶ Services, information

Figure 14   Business model C1: Services paid by the client

Business model C2: Embedded services

The service provider offers the services as part of (or "embedded in") another business transaction, such as hiring a tractor, buying seed or inputs, or selling produce.

Embedded services may also be subsidized or free, but we have no examples of these in this book.

Service provider
Private input supplier

Client
Farmers

→ Product
← Money
···▶ Services, information

Figure 15   Business model C2: Embedded services

The cases and the clusters

We have grouped the cases in Chapters 4–6 according to the three clusters (Table 3). Belonging to a particular cluster does not mean that the service provider uses only that model. Nor does it mean that this business model is its most important source of revenue. Our intention is rather to provide interesting and innovative examples for each cluster.

Table 3   Clusters of cases in this book

Cluster	Chapter	Cases, countries
Cluster A: Free services	4	Miruku, Mozambique 3C, Zambia DLSP, Uganda UGAMA CSC, Rwanda Excel Hort, Uganda
Cluster B: Subsidized services	5	Farmer training centres, Ethiopia Business service centres, Ghana Imbaraga, Rwanda
Cluster C: Fully paid by clients	6	Bindzu, Mozambique DADTCO, Mozambique ESDC, Uganda Target, Ethiopia

Main elements for analysis

We can analyse various aspects of these business service providers (and their business models) in terms of the relationships between the three key actors involved (clients, service providers, funders). We focus on four main elements in these relationships:

- **Financial sustainability** of the service provider and service provision

- **Accountability** of the service provider to the client

- Level of **inclusiveness** of the services

- **Capacity** strengthening needs of service providers.

The **financial sustainability** of the business service provider indicates the likelihood it can continue to operate in the future. Is the provider highly dependent on one donor or one client? Is it spreading its financial risks? The financial sustainability of the service provision is related to the project's or donor's exit strategy, which may (or may not) be in place. So are services needed for a longer period? If so, who can take over service provision? Or how can farmers pay directly for services after a project ends?

Accountability refers to the extent to which the clients (farmers, small enterprises or cooperatives) have a say about the type, costs and quality of the services they receive. Often, service providers are financially accountable only towards the funders; this is separate from their accountability for their performance and the services they deliver to the client. This triangular relation between funder, client and service provider will vary depending on the business model.

The **inclusiveness** of service provision refers to the extent to which the services manage to reach disadvantaged members of the population: the poor, women, young and elderly, and marginalized ethnic groups. It is often the result of a balance between the service provider's business orientation (for private providers), the funders' development vision, and the clients' organized articulation of demands.

The following chapters describe challenges and lessons about these aspects, derived both from the cases and the discussion among the writeshop participants.

A fourth element was particularly important in many of the cases: service providers lack the information and skills they need to do their work better. They can improve their capacity in two ways: by recruiting qualified staff, or by **strengthening the capacities** of existing staff. In general, it is difficult to recruit suitably qualified staff because such individuals have many other attractive job opportunities, and universities and training institutes do not produce enough people with the right skills. So we discuss how business providers can get the training, coaching and assistance they need to acquire the skills and competencies they need. The results of these discussions are found in Chapter 7.

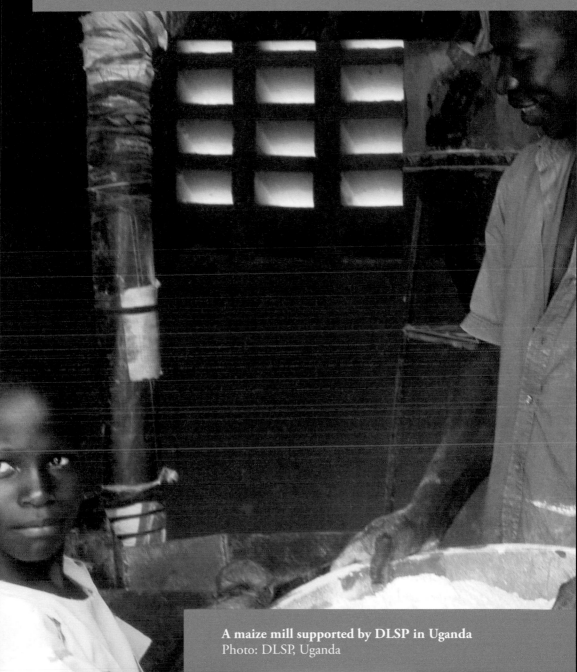

4 Cluster A:
Free services

A maize mill supported by DLSP in Uganda
Photo: DLSP, Uganda

4   Cluster A: Free services

In this cluster, farmers do not have to pay for the services they receive. The cost of providing the services is paid by someone else – the government, a development organization, or another actor in the value chain.

We describe five organizations whose major source of revenue fall into this category: Miruku in Mozambique, 3C in Zambia, and the District Livelihoods Support Programme (DLSP), UGAMA CSC and Excel Hort (all three in Uganda). Miruku, 3C and Excel Hort are private-sector providers; DLSP is a public provider; UGAMA is an NGO. Three of the cases reflect direct financing of the service provider (UGAMA, Miruku, 3C); DLSP is financed through tripartite agreements in which service providers, clients and donors work together.

Two other cases, Bindzu and Target, also provide services through a voucher system (or similar). They are described in Chapter 6.

Building competitiveness:
Miruku in Mozambique

Harvesting and quality control of cashew
Photo: Miruku, Mozambique

Building competitiveness:
Miruku in Mozambique

MIRUKU Lda. Sociedade Cooperativa de
Desenvolvimento e Serviços

Haje António

Why have so many development initiatives in northern Mozambique ended in failure? Part of the reason has been a lack of market studies, poorly defined strategies, inadequate organizational management, as well as deficient monitoring and evaluation. NGOs and other development organizations have simply not been prepared to work like, or with, businesses.

Founded in 2008 by a group of 11 professionals, Miruku Lda is trying to overcome these shortcomings. It provides a range of business services to small enterprises, NGOs,

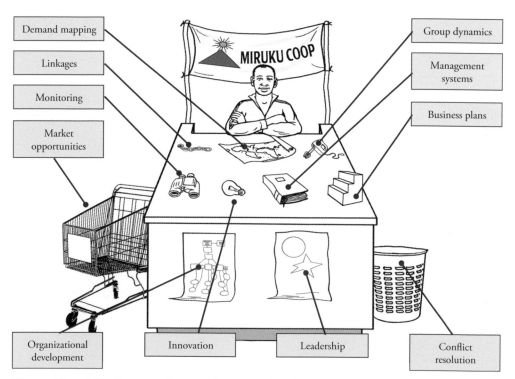

Figure 16   Miruku provides a wide range of services to its clients

development agencies and local governments. It helps small and medium enterprises to develop business plans based on market studies, establishes small-business-management systems, offers training in organizational development, and develops value-chain linkages. It assists NGOs, development organizations and public-sector agencies to design intervention strategies, and trains them on implementing projects. It supports the development of cooperatives and associations, and helps district governments to implement their local economic development strategies.

The word "Miruku" means "ideas" in Emakua, a language spoken in northern Mozambique. The company operates through short-term contracts (mostly studies, capacity building, short training courses) and medium-term contracts (0.5–3 years) for technical assistance and advice. It has five permanent staff members, and hires extra consultants when necessary.

In 2012, Miruku's turnover was an estimated $350,000. Sixty percent comes from the private sector (40% direct, and 20% originally from international donors but channelled through the private sector). Another 35% comes from an international donor (the Alliance for a Green Revolution in Africa, AGRA), and the remaining 5% from NGOs.

Examples of Miruku's work

Miruku is implementing a 3-year project funded by the **Alliance for a Green Revolution in Africa** to provide business development services to 80 small and medium enterprises serving 14,000 smallholders. It helps the enterprises gain business-planning and management skills, obtain credit, link to suppliers and buyers, and improve their management and operations.

Miruku helped the **Muecate Union** (a grouping of 20 farmers' associations with 400 individual groundnut and cashew producers) to get fair-trade certification. Miruku provided two types of assistance: organizational management (financial management, internal governance and transparency) and training (in fair trade principles, quality standards, production techniques and environmental conservation). The certification benefits the Muecate Union members: they get an additional MZN 2 (about 7 US cents) per kilogram, or about 15% more than what normal traders pay.

ProSavanna is a government programme to develop farming in the Nacala Development Corridor, which links the port of Nacala, in northern Mozambique, with landlocked Malawi and Zambia. **Oriental Consultant**, a Japanese company that is designing the master plan for ProSavanna, has asked Miruku for help. Miruku is taking stock of the farmers' associations active in the area, and is describing their farming systems. The findings and recommendations will contribute to thinking on how smallholder famers can be integrated into the region's large-scale development.

Miruku has provided a range of services for the **PRODEZA** programme, a Finnish-supported development project in Zambézia province. For example, it has worked with the local government on local economic development planning, and it has trained trainers in business planning and management for small entrepreneurs and farmers' associations.

Miruku has trained staff members of **Facilidade** (an NGO in Nampula province) and extensionists in agricultural business principles and tools such as budgeting and cost-benefit analysis. As a result, community members can now develop project proposals which are more market-oriented.

Miruku helped **AENA** (another NGO) in the coastal region of Nampula province with a small-scale fish-processing project. The 500 women involved in this project buy fish from local fishermen, clean them and sell them at the local market. Antonio Mutoua, operations director of AENA, says that this is one of the most promising projects he has seen. Miruku has also advised AENA how to transform market-oriented farmers' associations into cooperatives. That is important because under Mozambican law, associations are not allowed to have commercial operations. Cooperatives may do so.

IKURU is a private trading, processing and exporting company that is owned by farmers' associations, and private investors. The shareholders hired Miruku to help IKURU improve its management and to design a strategy and business plan. Miruku proposed an innovative structure, separating IKURU's business operations from its donor-funded social activities.

Business models

Miruku works through three different business models (Figure 17).

Business model A1: Government or donor pays for services to farmers

The current dominant business model is the one in which Miruku provides services for free for farmers. This accounts for 60% of the company's turnover, and is done in two slightly different ways.

In the first, international donors contract Miruku to train small and medium processors and nascent cooperatives to become competitive and integrated in their value chains. Miruku plays the role of a back-up provider of business services. This is a promising

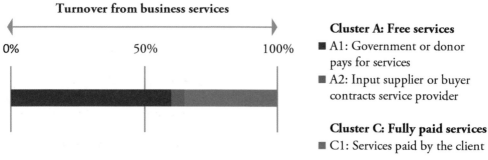

Turnover from business services

0%   50%   100%

Cluster A: Free services
■ A1: Government or donor pays for services
■ A2: Input supplier or buyer contracts service provider

Cluster C: Fully paid services
■ C1: Services paid by the client

Figure 17   **Share of business models in Miruku's revenue**

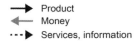

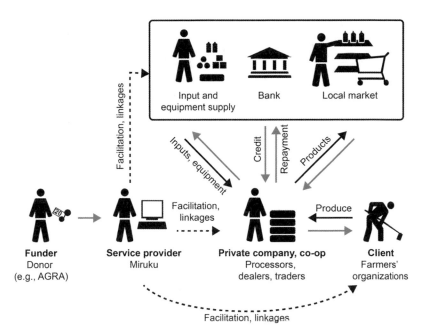

Figure 18   Miruku's business model A1 for its work with AGRA and the Muccate Union

model, according to Miruku, as it builds the clients' capacities to become independent from both donors' funding and from specific buyers. Miruku is investing its own resources in developing and testing this model further.

In the second variant, an NGO uses funds from a donor to hire Miruku to provide training to small and medium enterprises, local governments, civil-society organizations and producers' organizations. This variant is expected to become less important as Miruku is focusing on developing partnerships with the private sector.

Business model A2: Input supplier or buyer contracts service provider

In this model, Miruku is hired by a private-sector firm to provide services to others: small and medium enterprises and farmers. Its work for Oriental Consultant on the ProSavanna master plan falls into this category. Miruku helps these clients get ready to provide services (such as transport and catering) and agricultural products to the firm that hired it. This model accounts for only 5% of Miruku's revenues, but the company hopes it will grow as more big projects are implemented in Mozambique.

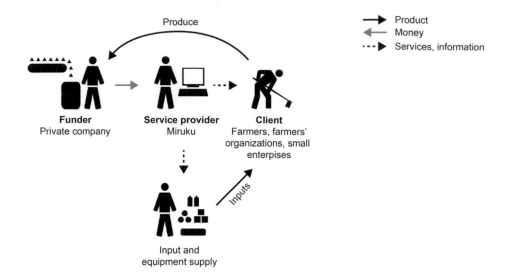

Figure 19   Miruku's business model A2 for its work on the ProSavanna master plan

Business model C1: Services paid by the client

Miruku also carries out research, market studies, training, business and strategy planning and reporting for other private companies. In 2011 this corresponded to 35% of the company's revenues. This model is particularly important because it allows Miruku to build the financial reserves to become more sustainable. A disadvantage is that the studies and research are often short-term.

Sustainability

Supporting farmers' organizations remains a challenge because the farmers do not yet pay for the cost of the assistance they receive. Many simply do not have the means to pay for Miruku's services. They need initial support to increase their productivity and income in order to bridge the gap between the cost of the services they get and the amount they can pay.

Miruku's financial sustainability is based on its clients' satisfaction. Many new projects come through references from previous clients. This reputation ensures that the company is often invited to meetings, seminars, etc., which are new opportunities for networking and meeting potential clients.

Miruku ensures that it stays in the market by providing innovative services to new projects or donors. To weather frequent changes, Miruku maintains a broad client base and a mix of short- and long-term contracts. This allows flexibility, ensures cash flow and reduces dependency on a single client. Miruku's current partnership with the Alliance for a Green Revolution in Africa will cover 70% of its basic costs (housing, communication, personnel) over the next 3 years. That allows Miruku space for reflection and innovation, and ensures its staff have the time to invest in developing new lines of work.

Inclusiveness

Miruku is committed to supporting local development, but it wants to do so in a commercial manner. In almost all its activities, Miruku supports organizations of smallholder farmers who manage 1–2 ha of land, as well as entrepreneurial farmers. Miruku is currently conducting needs assessments of farmers with the support of international NGOs such as Oxfam and Norges Vel. The idea is to provide technical support to such farmers and help them to get organized and reach the market. The AENA example illustrates how Miruku supports the development of women leaders.

Accountability

Where Miruku works with small and medium enterprises and other clients, it uses a form to get feedback about its services. When dealing with small-scale farmers, it uses meetings to do this. It also keeps in contact with the clients to understand how satisfied they are. The most concrete indicator of satisfaction is new assignments and contracts.

Challenges

Competition from international NGOs that offer similar services hurts Miruku. The company has to pay 17% tax on its services, but international NGOs are exempt. This is an example of how free competition can be distorted by non-private actors.

In the short term, it remains important for Miruku to have external funding so it can attend to the needs of small-scale farmers and help them become more entrepreneurial. But funding is useful only if it responds to the farmers' real needs and is in line with the market opportunities they have.

When it comes to small and medium enterprises, farmers' associations and individual entrepreneurs, though, it could be worthwhile to encourage them to purchase services. Some donor assistance or government support would be needed early in the process, followed by a gradual weaning away from external funding.

In the future, Miruku wants to continue to strengthen its relations with its current clients. It also wants to develop new services to meet market demands and clients' challenges. Its current effort to develop a line of work with entrepreneurial farmers is part of this trend.

Lessons

The reason for Miruku's relative success is a good reputation combined with a well-established network. Both are the result of staff skills and commitment. Miruku is one of the few private-sector providers in the region to offer these types of specialized services.

Miruku is interested in learning about new ways of providing farmers and other actors with services. It does so, in the first place, by investing its own resources in courses and education. In addition, it looks for opportunities to learn from similar experiences elsewhere, such as the writeshop that gave origin to this book.

More information

Agri-Hub Mozambique. Promovendo o Empreendedorismo dos Agricultores. http:// apf-mozambique.ning.com

Dzimba, D., E. Kirjasniemi, R. Paterson, A. Ribeiro, A. Tcheco, L. Vaaranmaa, S. Värttö, P. de Carvalho, and E. 2010. Neves. PRODEZA. Strengthening the foundations of sustainable rural development in Zambézia. Rural Development in Zambézia Province Project (PRODEZA). http://tinyurl.com/cqeo3z6

Chissungue Haje António, haje.miruku@gmail.com, miruku@tdm.co.mz

Balancing the interests of donors and clients: 3C in Zambia

Balancing the interests of donors and clients: 3C in Zambia

Catherine Phiri

The HIV/AIDS pandemic has hit many rural households in Zambia hard, making it very difficult for them to earn a living. The government and development organizations help them cope in various ways. One is to help people, especially the young and women, to form groups to develop farm enterprises. These enable their members to earn money by growing and marketing maize, groundnuts, horticultural produce, honey and dried bananas. Local NGOs support the community groups to develop these enterprises.

3C Development Management and Entrepreneurship Experts Ltd is a private-sector service provider founded in 2008 by three Zambian consultants. It is one of the organizations that the government and donors have contracted to identify the areas where NGOs need to improve, then deliver training and coaching. 3C trains the NGO staff (as well as farmers' groups) in group management and preparing business plans. It mentors them on management issues (for example through regular field visits and email and telephone contacts), and helps them put their plans into effect.

Most of 3C's business services are tailor-made for each client. But as the company gains experience, it has become increasingly possible to standardize some aspects, such as needs assessment, strategic planning and entrepreneurship training. That makes providing the services cheaper.

The Youth Development Association in Kawambwa district, Luapula Province is one of the NGOs supported by 3C. It in turn serves around 15 community groups in its area. Over a period of about 2 years, 3C staff helped the association develop its capacity to offer training on group entrepreneurship and business planning. Other 3C clients include the Zambia Governance Foundation, various Finnish development organizations, Care International, the International Labour Organization (ILO), the United States Agency for International Development (USAID) and the Ministry of Agriculture and Livestock.

3C has developed a cadre of competent business service providers and has helped set up an association of such providers and an accreditation scheme for them. It has also coordinated the establishment of institutes for entrepreneurship and organizational development. 3C staff have trained many individuals, including those linked to the African Union's Comprehensive Africa Agriculture Development Programme in Zambia. It is currently coordinating a network of individuals trained under this programme. These activities make 3C a back-up service provider – one that supports and strengthens other service providers.

Clients appreciate the 3C facilitators' ability to motivate them and help change their mindset to a more entrepreneurial orientation. They also like 3C's professional management support, particularly in financial management and the use of local languages. 3C is initiating a computerized knowledge-management system that will report on the services it delivers, results obtained and level of client satisfaction.

Business models

3C delivers its services mainly through three different business models: direct financing by government and development partners (85% of turnover), paid assignments from private companies, and wealthy individuals (10% of turnover), and partial payment by farmers (5% of turnover) (Figure 20).

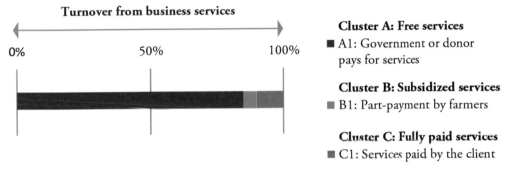

Figure 20   Share of business models in 3C's revenue

Business model A1: Government or donor pays for services to farmers

Most (85%) of 3C's revenue comes from providing a range of services to local NGOs and community organizations such as cooperatives and individual farmer groups. This work is financed by the government and by donors such as USAID and ILO.

Figure 21   3C's business model A1

Business model C1: Services paid by the client

3C provides business planning and technical assistance to clients such as larger-scale farmers, wealthy individuals and private companies for a fee. This accounts for 10% of 3C's revenue.

Business model B1: Part-payment by farmers

3C is exploring ways to charge small-scale farmers and their organizations for at least part of the costs of the services they receive. This model now represents only 5% of the turnover, but is likely to grow.

Sustainability

3C has won tenders for donor-funded contracts to support rural groups, and is heavily dependent on this type of funding. The company is trying to diversify its finance by exploring new markets for its services. Private-sector operators and the urban middle classes interested in farming increasingly contact 3C for services. In the short term, 3C sees itself as continuing to depend on development agencies, but in the longer term, other clients are expected to come in. As medium and large private-sector actors emerge in specific value chains, they are approaching 3C for services such as developing business plans for how to best procure, process and market agricultural produce.

Smallholder farmer groups may contribute towards the costs of some business services they see as vital. A survey conducted by 3C in Nyimba district found that farmers are willing to pay for training on new production techniques, processing and marketing. 3C is currently exploring whether it can respond to this new demand.

A growing segment of the urban middle class is moving into agribusiness. These people form a potential market for 3C's business services since they have cash and are interested in farming, but lack the experience to do it properly.

Inclusiveness

Through the business models A1 and B1, 3C has mainly worked with disadvantaged rural groups such as women, young people, the disabled and people affected by HIV. This emphasis is determined by donors and government. The company foresees an increasing emphasis on entrepreneurial farmers and on fast-growing and export-oriented agricultural enterprises.

Accountability

3C is typically part of a three-way relationship with funding agencies and primary clients (such as a local NGO or farmer group). The ultimate target group (rural households) are

> **Box 5   Policy changes in Zambia encouraging the growth of private-sector business development services**
> - Zambia Development Agency Act (2006)
> - Citizens Economic Empowerment Act (2006)
> - Micro, Small and Medium Enterprise Policy (2009)
> - Banking and Financial Services Act (2000)
> - Zambia National Agriculture Policy (2004–15)
> - National Policy on Environment (2009)

scarcely involved. In practice the funding agency holds the purse-strings and decides what types of services the clients should receive. The clients are thus often passive recipients of services. 3C is aware of this dilemma, and puts a lot of effort in balancing the requirements of donors and the needs of its clients. 3C conducts formal evaluations (during training and coaching programmes), but also relies on informal feedback.

Challenges

The government of Zambia has contributed to an enabling environment for business services in a number of ways. It has put less priority on government-run extension services, and opened up opportunities and incentives for private-sector players in providing services. Box 5 lists some of the relevant laws and policy changes.

Things do not always go smoothly, as illustrated by the Zambia Development Agency's now-discontinued voucher scheme. Under this scheme, farmers received vouchers they could use to pay for services from business service providers. The providers took these vouchers to a fund manager in exchange for cash. This was fine in theory. But in practice, there were complaints that vouchers were not distributed fairly or transparently to farmers. It was alleged that some farmers who got vouchers were pressured to go to particular service providers. Some farmers may have connived with service providers and shared the money once the vouchers were cashed. Overall, the roles of government, the private sector and development organizations did not appear clearly defined. As a result, the scheme failed.

The country still needs a clear policy framework for business services. This would create a basis for coordination among the various players, sharing of lessons and promoting the sector as a whole. 3C has been working with Mulungushi University to study how to improve the stakeholders' roles.

Lessons

Providing effective business service requires two sets of skills: agricultural production and entrepreneurship development. Few local consultants combine these skills. More needs to be done to create a group of people who have the knowledge and skills to develop businesses in practice.

Figure 22   3C's service delivery to farmers depends on suitable government policies

When 3C started work, facilitating access to financial services was one of its major focuses. But few development agencies in Zambia have paid attention to this topic. This neglect has harmed 3C's portfolio and turnover, and seems to delay agribusiness development as a whole.

In supporting the organizational development of rural NGOs, donors pay relatively little attention to agribusiness entrepreneurship. 3C and other business service providers need to do more to demonstrate that this is an important and promising area for NGOs, making their work more relevant for rural communities.

More information

http://apf-finance.ning.com/profile/ChristianChileshe

Christian Chileshe, principal consultant, entrepreneurship development, 3C Development Management & Entrepreneurship Experts Ltd., cchileshe.3c@gmail.com

Enterprise grants in Uganda: The District Livelihoods Support Programme

Careful records are vital in managing a business
Photo: DLSP, Uganda

Enterprise grants in Uganda: The District Livelihoods Support Programme

JLIFAD

Enabling poor rural people
to overcome poverty

Adeline Muheebwa

Local governments in Uganda help farmers' groups by providing them with a range of free enterprise development services: training, demonstrations, farmer-to-farmer extension and participation in trade shows. These activities are funded from the regular government budget, the Local Government Fund, and development partners and projects. One such project is the District Livelihoods Support Programme (DLSP), funded by the International Fund for Agricultural Development (IFAD) and the Ugandan government.

One of DLSP's goals is to overcome hurdles facing enterprise development. DLSP helps rural households improve their income and food security while enabling local governments to deliver relevant services to them. It has set up learning centres at host-farmers' premises to demonstrate new technologies. For the poorest people, the programme offers special grants to improve their food security. It also offers enterprise grants, a one-off form of support to farmers' groups to help their transition from subsistence to commercial agriculture. The targets of the enterprise grants are intermediate-level groups of farmers who already have some knowledge about farming and are involved in income-generation and savings-and-credit schemes.

To apply for the enterprise grant, a group must prepare a viable, competitive business proposal. Each grant may be up to $5,000 (USh 13.5 million), depending on the type of enterprise. The enterprises supported fall into three types:

- **Household.** The enterprise given to the group may be managed by each household. Many of the livestock and crop enterprises fall into this category: each group member may raise his or her own cows and goats, or plantation of bananas, coffees or pineapples. For livestock the "pass on" method is used: members who receive a female animal pass on a calf or kid to someone else in the group. Enterprises that produce livestock and crops are managed best by this model.

- **Cluster.** In this model, the group members cluster into manageable sizes and run the enterprise, either together or in turns. Enterprises using this model include animal traction (oxen, a plough and perhaps a weeder and a cart), livestock and beekeeping.

- **Group.** The enterprise is managed by all the group members who are represented by the executive committee members. For example, the group may start a maize mill and run it as a joint enterprise. Most of the enterprises that process produce or add value have been

The business of agricultural business services

group-based; they have generally been very effective. The grants for such enterprises tend to be larger because they have to cover costly items like buildings and machinery. A few group enterprises grow crops or raise livestock or bees.

DLSP establishes learning centres at selected host farmers' premises to demonstrate new technologies. They function as the sites for farmer-to-farmer learning and group meetings, as well as making it possible to organize visits to other farms and trade shows. They serve a broad range of farmers, not just those in the DLSP-supported groups.

Since its start in 2007, the programme has provided more than 600 such grants. Box 6 describes how the programme works in one district, Bugiri.

Business models

Business model A1: Government or donor pays for services to farmers

This is DLSP's most important model: the farmers get free services, funded by the Ugandan government and a donor programme.

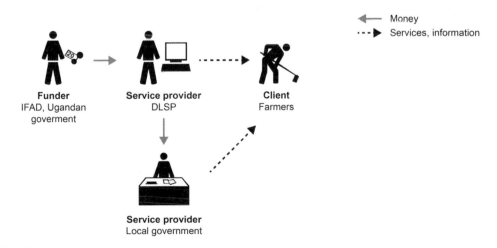

Figure 23   DLSP's business model A1

Business model B1: Part-payment by farmers

Sometimes the community members pay a part of the cost of the services that DLSP provides. This, however, represents only a small part of DLSP's operations.

Figure 24   DLSP's business model B1

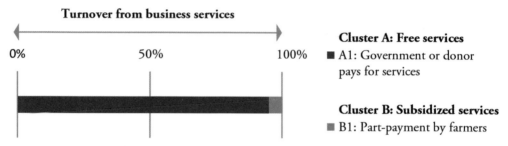

Figure 25   Share of business models in DLSP's enterprise grants programme

Results

Investing profits. Farmers' groups invest the revenues from their enterprise in existing and new businesses (Box 7).

Building capacity. The group members have learned various business skills: how to run an enterprise, plan a business, get and use market information, and keep records. They have also learned improved farm practices.

Increased trust. Transparent records make it more likely that the group members will trust each other more. That helps avoid conflicts and makes the group stronger.

Working as a group. Non-members increasingly acknowledge the benefits of working in a group. When DSLP started, many farmers were sceptical and did not want to take part. Now the enterprises are established, more and more farmers want to join in.

Food security. There is now less risk of food shortages. Instead of selling their unmilled maize they now increasingly mill their maize to make flour for home consumption or to sell.

The business of agricultural business services

Box 7 Idohwe group members profit from a maize mill

The Idohwe Disabled Development Association used its enterprise grant to set up a maize mill. This enables members to make posho, a local staple dish.

Lydia, the group's finance secretary, used to sell her maize as grain. She would sell around 1,500 kg each season at USh 400 per kilogram, earning her USh 600,000 (about $220). She now grinds her grain using the group's mill. She can make about 1,000 kg of flour, which she sells at USh 2,000 per kilogram. The milling costs USh 70 per kilogram, leaving her with an income of USh 1,930/kg, or USh 1,930,000 (about $720) in all.

The Idohwe group has expanded its business by winning orders to supply maize flour to nearby schools. The maize grown in the community now has a steady market, so local farmers can increase their production. The group wants to invest profits from the mill in setting up a poultry unit. This would use by-products from the milling as feed.

Savings and loans. Many groups run small savings-and-loans schemes. They use these to save and reinvest the profits from their enterprises.

Sustainability

The DSLP enterprise grants help farmers establish businesses that improve their incomes. As local government services have improved, demand for them has gone up. As their businesses grow and generate income, farmers are able to pay for these services. For example, livestock keepers can now pay for veterinary services and drugs.

While DLSP is due to end in 2 years' time, the provision of services is sustainable because it uses the government structures, which will remain in place.

Inclusiveness

DLSP has two types of grants for the different categories of farmers: enterprise grants for those who are shifting to commercial farming, and food-security grants for poorer households.

The enterprise-grant scheme requires that at least 30% of the group members are women, and at least 30% of the leaders must also be women. This requirement has increased women's empowerment in the community, and more women are taking part in the programme.

Accountability

A farmers' group contributes at least 20% of the resources required for the enterprise it established with its DLSP's enterprise grant. This enhances the group's feeling of ownership

**Figure 26   DLSP uses the Gender Action Learning System methodology to empha-
size gender justice and ownership**

for the enterprise. The business idea comes from the farmers, and it is they who develop a business plan and a fundable proposal. The farmers, not DLSP, are solely responsible for managing the enterprise.

Government officials, the donor and the project staff jointly monitor the farmers' groups and their enterprises. They make regular field visits to the districts and to the groups to review progress, interact with the members and get their feedback. DLSP provides continued training and coaching during these visits. The farmers' groups also monitor progress. The group members are trained how to keep transparent records, so ensuring accountability.

Challenges

The enterprise grant scheme faces various challenges.

Bureaucracy. Since DLSP is a government programme, a lot of bureaucracy and paperwork are involved. In the past this led to long delays in implementation: although the programme was launched in 2007, the first grant in Bugiri was made only in 2009–10. A revision in the programme design also caused delays. The procurement procedures are quite lengthy and involve a number of processes: from advertising for bids to supply inputs, to distributing them to the farmers. That pushes up transaction costs.

Funding. DLSP has found it difficult to ensure it has enough money to run the enterprise programme. The exchange rate between the Ugandan shilling and the US dollar fluctuates, which may mean that the farmers' groups get less than anticipated. Transport is a large cost, and there are limited resources to pay for follow-up visits to monitor and guide activities in the field.

Raised expectations. Handing out grants can raise unrealistic expectations among group members, especially as DLSP is a government programme. The beneficiaries tend to want more, and they expect immediate benefits. The farmers may get disappointed and lose motivation if they do not see these. It takes time and sensitization to change their mindset.

Ensuring fair distribution of benefits. Ensuring that all group members benefit from the enterprise grant can be difficult. For instance, a grant for cattle-rearing can buy only a small number of cows. It can take years before they have given birth to enough calves for everyone in the group to benefit from the grant. This affects the group's commitment and may leave some group members more enthusiastic than others. To overcome this challenge, DLSP makes more enterprise grants for value-addition enterprises (such as maize mills), which serve all members and whose revenues can be invested further or shared among the members. Alternatively, DLSP encourages more individual enterprises (like goat-raising), where each member gets his or her own animals and manages them individually. There is no insurance to cover theft or loss (for example, if an animal dies), and the group will not be compensated if this happens.

An enabling environment. This is important for the development of local enterprises. It includes tax policies, a free and stable environment for interaction between public services and private providers, government staff with business knowledge and orientation, and a market orientation of the government's advisory services. All these affect the management and sustainability of the enterprises.

Lessons

Using established structures. There are benefits of implementing a programme through the government: structures are in place from village to national level. Government staff with various skills can implement the programme.

Importance of trainers. It is important to have good trainers and to continuously improve their ability to train.

Women's participation. Women are committed to group enterprises, but they have to be actively included in managing and running them.

Building capacity. Group enterprises are a good way of building members' capacities and allowing them to put what they learn into practice. Members who are the most active in their groups tend to benefit more and often help others to learn; they become model entrepreneurs in the community.

More information

www.molg.go.ug/projects/dlsp

Adeline Muheebwa, ademuheebwa@gmail.com

Moving from a development to a business approach: UGAMA CSC, Rwanda

UGAMA staff giving a training course for members of a start-up cooperative
Photo: UGAMA, Rwanda

Moving from a development to a business approach: UGAMA CSC, Rwanda

J. Richard N. Kanyarukiga and Innocent Simpunga

Cooperatives are a key feature of the agricultural landscape in Rwanda. They deal with a wide range of areas such as crop and livestock production, input supply, processing, marketing, training and financial services. Cooperatives provide a wider range of services to their members. But they face many challenges. Some lack skills in record-keeping, accountancy, planning, sourcing supplies and marketing. Others find it hard to get information on new techniques or emerging market opportunities. Where can they go for help?

The answer is UGAMA CSC. This NGO was founded through a project led by COOPIBO, a Belgian development agency. Its job then was to help farmers and other rural people to form cooperatives. At the end of the project, UGAMA CSC continued on its own. It was officially registered in 1985 as an independent organization. It still helps local people create cooperatives, but a large part of its work is now to support those that already exist. Currently it serves 26 cooperatives.

UGAMA operates in Rwanda's Southern Province, where it maintains a permanent presence in Muhanga, Kamonyi and Ruhango districts. In each district it coordinates its work with the local government and other rural development organizations through the district's Joint Action Development Forum.

Groups that want to join UGAMA's programmes just have to ask: the application procedure is simple. UGAMA then visits the group and checks on its needs and areas for potential assistance. Its research unit also identifies poor communities that may require support, and designs appropriate interventions. UGAMA is currently working in 10 such communities, where it runs demonstration plots and helps farmers improve their production, handling, processing and marketing of crops such as maize, wheat, rice, potatoes and mushrooms. These communities are on track to forming their own cooperatives.

In the future, UGAMA aims to strengthen the maize, rice and coffee value chains, and to help its client cooperatives become champions in sustainable development. UGAMA will need extra money to do this: it is hiring experienced staff to strengthen its fundraising activities.

Figure 27   As farmers' groups grow, their needs for business services change

Services

UGAMA's work focuses on three broad areas:

- **Improved agricultural techniques.** UGAMA supports cooperatives by promoting sustainable agriculture, and helping them improve their farming practices and marketing. It focuses both on small-scale production for subsistence as well as larger-scale farming for the market.

- **Small-scale processing technologies.** This aims to add value to products, for example by making juice and sweets from pineapples, making cooking oil from soybeans and sunflower, turning soybeans into tofu and soy milk, and milling cassava and rice. This activity also includes advice on packaging, standards, marketing, etc.

- **Financial services.** Many of the cooperatives that UGAMA serves have savings-and-loan schemes for their members. UGAMA helps them prepare business plans, apply for loans from commercial lenders, and manage their businesses in a professional manner.

UGAMA delivers its services in various ways. It offers training on request to individual cooperatives, as well as courses that are open to members of different farmer groups. Every three years it conducts a needs-assessment among its clients, and designs training programmes and other interventions to respond to the needs identified. Many of its courses are "training of trainers" where lead farmers are trained who will pass on their new knowledge to other farmers.

It also acts as an information source for its clients on subjects such as crop production and new varieties, standards, potential markets and the sources of funding. It links its clients to other stakeholders, such as research institutes and consultancy firms.

Business models

Business model A1: Government or donor pays for services to farmers

Every three years, UGAMA prepares a strategic plan that describes what it hopes to do in the coming period. It then approaches international donors (such as ICCO, Pain pour le Monde, Protos and the Canadian Cooperative Association). When it has secured funding, it can execute its plan and provide services to the cooperatives and local communities.

Under this model, UGAMA provides services such as cost–benefit analysis, market linkages, business planning, coaching on strategic planning, management tools, farm management techniques, financial management control, seed and product certification, and linkage to research technologies.

UGAMA also responds to requests from donors and development agencies to provide services for their programmes. Here the initiative comes from the funder, not UGAMA. Typical services include coaching on value chains, training, organizing cooperatives,

←	Money
---▶	Services, information

Funder
International donor

Service provider
UGAMA

Client
Cooperatives,
community members

Figure 28   UGAMA's business model A1

business planning, strategic planning, and facilitating agribusiness clusters. If it does not have the expertise itself, UGAMA hires consultants to do the job. UGAMA offers these services outside the three districts where it has permanent representatives.

Business model A1 accounts for about 90% of UGAMA's business-service revenue.

Business models C1 (services paid by client) and A3 (vouchers)

Mature cooperatives sometimes request UGAMA for assistance in things such as business planning, external auditing, and planning new ventures. UGAMA charges the cooperative a fee for such services. The cooperative may pay UGAMA's fees from its own members' fees (business model C1), or may apply to the government-run "basket fund", a pot of money available to cooperatives for development activities (model A3). These two models account for about 10% of UGAMA's business-service revenue.

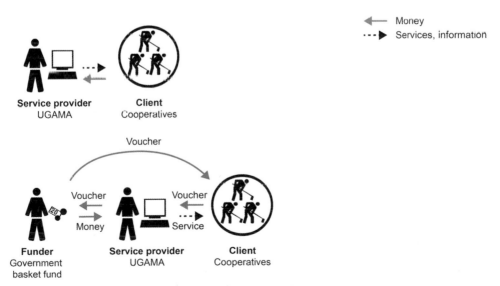

←	Money
---▶	Services, information

Service provider
UGAMA

Client
Cooperatives

Voucher

Voucher

Funder
Government
basket fund

Voucher

Money

Service provider
UGAMA

Voucher

Service

Client
Cooperatives

Figure 29   UGAMA's business models C1 (top) and A3 (bottom)

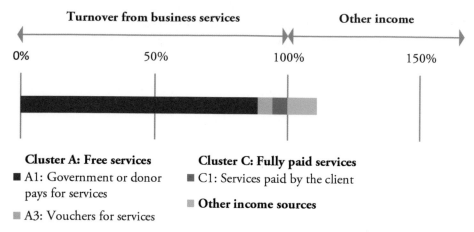

Figure 30   Share of business models in UGAMA CSC's revenue

Other sources of income

UGAMA has started to invest in companies by taking equity in them. It has a 20% share in APISCO, a firm that supplies agricultural inputs. The other shareholder is IABM, a cooperative it supports. APISCO supplies inputs to rice farmers, who sell their output to a miller in which UGAMA also has a 20% stake. The other shareholder in the miller is COPRORIZ, another cooperative that UGAMA supports. As an NGO, under Rwandan law UGAMA is allowed to make such investments. It uses the revenue to support its running costs and to use as counterpart funding to attract donor finance for its social programmes. UGAMA is interested in expanding its investment portfolio to other companies.

Results

Some examples of the impacts of UGAMA's work:

• COPRORIZ, a cooperative of rice producers in Kamonyi district, has 2,750 members (60% of them women). They have raised their yields from 3 to 8 tons per hectare as a result of UGAMA's training, mentoring visits and the introduction of new rice varieties. UGAMA helped COPRORIZ write a business plan for a mill and get a loan for this from the Kenya Commercial Bank. The mill started operations in early 2012.

• IABM, a 764-member cooperative in Muhanga district, has raised its maize yields from 3 tons to 5 tons per hectare. It increased its rice purchases to 480 tons in 2011. It has become a shareholder in APISCO, an input-supply company operating in Southern Province, and has opened a shop where members can buy supplies.

• CODDT, a cooperative of maize and rice producers, has improved its internal organization and got officially registered. It more than tripled its turnover from RwF 11 million ($18,000) in 2008 to RwF 37 million ($60,000) in 2009. In 2011, the annual turnover reached RwF 52.8 million ($85,160).

- UGAMA was instrumental in linking cooperatives to the government's Agriculture Board, which buys certified seed and distributes it to farmers throughout the country. Producing seed was a new, highly profitable business for the cooperatives.

Surveys of cooperatives and individual farmers indicate high levels of satisfaction with UGAMA. Farmers acknowledge their progress is a direct result of UGAMA's training and facilitation, including facilitating access to financial support.

Sustainability

UGAMA has grown steadily from a budget of $100,000 in 1985 to $600,000 in 2012. The trend clearly has been upwards. Cooperatives play a central role in the Rwandan government's development policies. UGAMA complements the work of the government's Rwanda Cooperative Agency.

UGAMA foresees a growing demand for its services from cooperatives. As cooperatives mature, the types of services they need change. UGAMA is well-placed to provide the sorts of services that they require and are prepared to pay for. At the same time, UGAMA has diversified its income base to consultancy services and direct investment in production and processing companies. This promises stability in the future.

Inclusiveness

UGAMA's services are open to all members of the cooperatives; the vast majority of such people are poor. UGAMA sets aside part of its resources specifically to help disadvantaged communities by setting up demonstration sites, helping them form their own cooperatives, and ensuring that they benefit from their services.

Accountability

UGAMA is accountable to its funders, the government and clients in various ways:

- UGAMA involves its clients in planning, implementing, monitoring and evaluating its activities. It signs tripartite contracts with the donor and the client, and holds regular quarterly meetings with the local stakeholders to check on progress and adjust activities.

- The cooperatives that UGAMA serves have set up a joint control committee to monitor, evaluate and provide feedback on UGAMA's work.

- UGAMA reports regularly on progress to the district government's Joint Action District Forum, where all main stakeholders meet.

- UGAMA reports back to its donors and other stakeholders on progress in relation to its 3-year action plan. These reports contain evidence of progress made.

Challenges

The demand for UGAMA's services greatly exceeds the organization's ability to deliver them. There are two big problems: technical and financial.

UGAMA does not have sufficient staff with the right qualifications to deliver the services required. It is recruiting new specialists to fill this gap. It has initiated a partnership with local universities to train the graduates in rural development topics, and to use their expertise to deliver services to their clients. It uses these trainees as volunteers in the field. UGAMA also trains lead farmers, who then pass on their knowledge to their fellow cooperative members.

In terms of finance, UGAMA is trying to attract more donor funding by strengthening its fundraising unit. It is also building up its own capital by investing in property and processing companies. It is developing its consultancy department to generate more income from new customers.

The government's role is generally positive, but interference can be a problem. For example, it tends to push people into cooperatives in a top-down manner, and wants UGAMA to help organize them. But UGAMA's approach is more bottom-up: it helps local people identify their needs, and then decide whether a cooperative is an appropriate way to fulfil those needs.

Lessons

Approaches to providing business services are changing. The development approach, where donors fund projects that support farmers, is gradually giving way to a business approach, where the aim is to stimulate profitable enterprises. The same logic applies to actors in the value chain and to service providers. This implies tensions between NGOs, which are development-oriented and typically rely on donor funding, and profit-oriented service providers, which are business-oriented and rely on income they can generate from clients that directly pay for the services they provide.

It can be difficult for organizations like UGAMA to find an exit strategy as their clients approach maturity. Clients that are used to getting free or subsidized services may be reluctant to pay the full cost. It is expected that after a transaction period the cooperatives will be willing to pay for the services they really appreciate and need.

More information

www.ugamacsc.org.rw

J. Richard N. Kanyarukiga, jrnkanyarukiga@yahoo.com
Innocent Simpunga, simpungai@yahoo.fr, ugamacsc@rwanda1.com

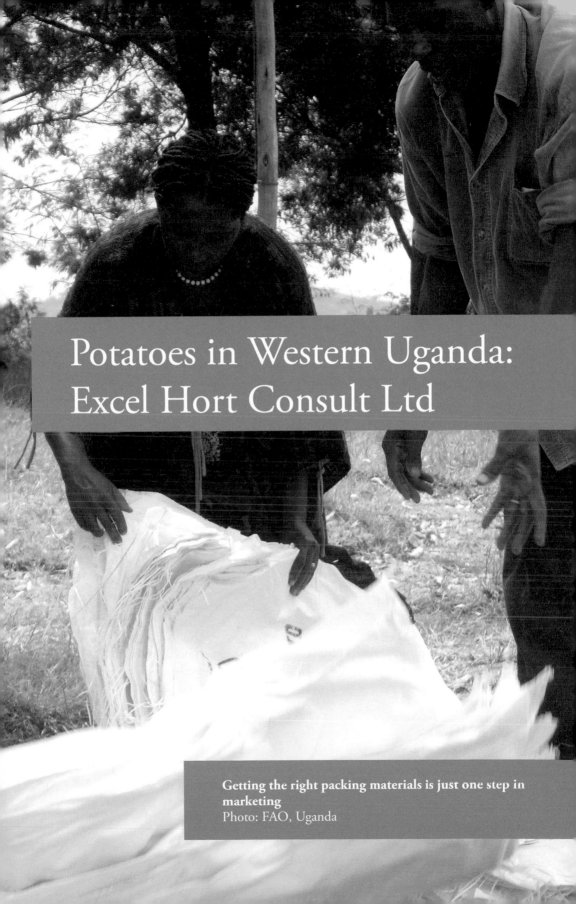

Potatoes in Western Uganda: Excel Hort Consult Ltd

Getting the right packing materials is just one step in marketing
Photo: FAO, Uganda

Potatoes in Western Uganda: Excel Hort Consult Ltd

Alex Ariho and May Murungi

Edson, a potato farmer in western Uganda, used to sell his crop to a local trader, who gave him a mere $19 a bag. But now the same bag fetches $27. Edson's output has more than doubled too, from 15 bags to 30 a season.

What has made the difference? Edson and his neighbours have formed a marketing association so they can sell their produce as a group. That saves on transport costs and enables them to sell to a more lucrative market in Kampala, the distant capital. It also means they can get good-quality, certified seed potatoes and other inputs, as well as credit and technical advice. All these services are available to a group, but are hard for individual farmers like Edson to get.

Marketing associations have a lot of advantages, but they rarely form by themselves. It usually takes some kind of outside stimulus to help farmers get organized. And they need assistance to create an organization that functions and provides services efficiently to its members.

Helping form and guide such marketing groups was the task of Excel Hort Consult Ltd as part of a big project led by the Food and Agriculture Organization of the United Nations (FAO). Founded in 1999, this agribusiness development company provides value chain development services to local, national and international organizations as well as to the private sector. Excel Hort works with farmer groups on group mobilization, capacity building, and information and marketing networks.

Excel Hort currently employs 30 professionals and operates in 29 districts in Uganda. It is headquartered in Mbarara. As its name indicates, the company started out with a focus on horticulture. But 5 years later, a strategic review revealed a rising demand for agribusiness services and private-sector companies to steer economic development. That is where the company's focus is now.

Excel Hort offers a wide range of services: agribusiness and horticulture value chain analysis and development, market information services, project and programme design, implementation and evaluations, impact assessments, strategic planning and institutional development, as well as business management services, procurement and contract management, corporate identity development and branding. All its services are designed to enhance capacity development and poverty reduction through strengthening the private sector.

Three stages

Its work for the FAO project is an example of what Excel Hort does. It fell in three stages:

Mobilization. Excel Hort helped the farmers organize themselves into producer groups, and strengthened existing groups. It trained them in group dynamics, introduced the project's approach, and assisted them in planning activities. It also supported the groups to form second-tier marketing associations, one for each sub-county.

Capacity building. Excel Hort trained and mentored the farmer groups and marketing associations on subjects such as postharvest handling and storage, record-keeping, group dynamics, agronomic practices, collective marketing, sorting, grading and bulking. The programme also included training of trainers, where selected members learned skills that they could pass on to others in the group.

Information and marketing networks. Public information boards were set up at the marketing associations and other places in each sub-county. These boards are also used to advertise products and current prices and to display announcements. The manager of each board gets the price information via mobile phone and puts it on the board for all to see. The manager also gets SMS messages from AgriNet, an agribusiness company that supplies such information. Excel Hort linked the farmer groups and associations to seed producers, seed certifiers, input suppliers, financial institutions, buyers and traders. Many of these linkages were cemented through a contract or memorandum of understanding. Although Excel Hort established the linkages, it is now up to the farmers to sustain them.

Results

The Excel Hort component of the FAO project focused on three districts, two of which, Kabale and Kisoro, grow potatoes. Excel Hort helped the farmers add value and process their crop, and empowered them through training and information sharing. It served 739 households, grouped into 24 groups in the two districts.

Excel Hort arranged a series of meetings between the farmers and restaurants in Kampala. That led to a contract between a marketing association in Kabale district and Nandos, a big fast-food restaurant in the city centre. The marketing association sorts the potatoes and sells the bigger ones to Nandos. The contract assures the farmers of a good market and a fixed price: their income no longer depends on the variable prices offered by traders.

Potato production rose as a result, from just over 4,000 bags in May 2009 to nearly 14,000 bags just one season later, in October in the same year. This increase was due to the better production practices the farmers learned through training and the inputs they have been able to get.

Excel Hort uses local government staff to provide services such as training courses for farmers. It also works with others, such as certified seed producers, farm-input dealers, buyers and financial institutions. Linking farmers to these players is a key element of the project.

Business models

Excel Hort has three main business models. It offers free services to clients, paid for by donors and governments. It provides services that are contracted and paid for by the client. And it processes and sells products. Its turnover is $300,000 a year.

Business model A1: Government or donor pays for services to farmers

Free services to farmers can take different forms: Excel Hort manages a project or programme on behalf of a donor and charges a percentage of the budget as management fee. It provides services to farmers such as training in business management skills, group formation and governance, packing and labelling, value addition, collective marketing and linking farmers to input suppliers, financial institutions and to markets. It collaborates with the local government to implement these projects. The FAO project described above is an example of this. This model accounts for 80% or more of Excel Hort's business-service turnover.

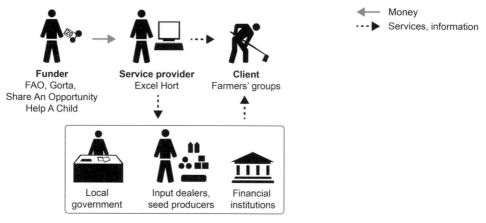

Figure 31   Excel Hort's business model A1

Business model C1: Services paid by the client

Excel Hort also provides consultancy services on value chains, business development and marketing to large-scale entrepreneurs or cooperatives. It charges a fee for these services. If it cannot provide specialized services itself, it subcontracts other providers to do so. Examples include tractor services and irrigation systems. This model accounts for under 20% of its business-service turnover.

The business of agricultural business services

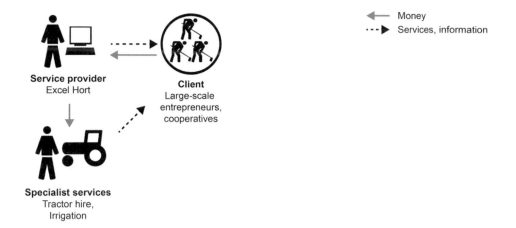

Figure 32   Excel Hort's business model C1

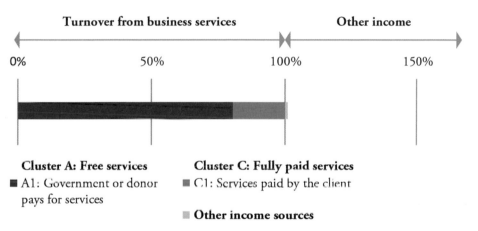

Figure 33   Share of business models in Excel Hort's revenue

Other sources of income

Finally, Excel Hort has a production department that buys tree tomatoes from producers and processes them into wine for sale. This line of business has just been started, so contributes little to turnover. The plan is for Excel Hort to grow its own tree tomatoes to increase production.

Sustainability

Excel Hort does not rely on a single source of income or business model: it has various clients and an expanding range of business. It also earns money in other ways, such as its tree-tomato winemaking enterprise.

Within the potato project, Excel Hort is trying to make the services self-sustaining. The farmers can now produce their own seed and get it certified. Some have been trained as trainers, so can provide certain types of services to other group members. The groups set their membership fees themselves; the money pays for the group activities. The marketing associations can get loans from financial institutions so they can finance their trading activities.

Most of the services that Excel Hort provides are paid for by the FAO-managed grant. The recipients have to make a contribution to the activity, but not to Excel Hort. When groups start up, Excel Hort helps them draw up a constitution that sets membership fees and rules, a code of conduct and sanctions for group members.

Farmers are supposed to contribute to the market information boards: if they use the information on the boards, they have to pay a fee. Because the members sell their potatoes through the marketing association, it knows the volume sold using the information. The boards have space for local news, announcements and advertisements (which the advertiser pays for).

Nevertheless, it is hard to get people to pay for the information services. The government provides the original data for free, so the groups do not see why they should pay for them – even though it costs money to collate the data and maintain the boards.

Figure 34   Market information boards display prices, news and announcements

The business of agricultural business services

Accountability

Excel Hort is accountable to its clients in various ways. When it provides consultancy services to private entrepreneurs, it receives a management fee and is held accountable through monitoring and evaluation by the funder. Excel Hort strives to maintain a good reputation with its various clients so it can get new contracts with both entrepreneurs and donors.

In the potato project, Excel Hort is accountable to its clients (the farmers' groups and marketing associations), the donor, and the government. It uses participatory evaluation tools at different stages of the project. Farmers use these tools to keep track of progress and to ensure that the services they receive are good-quality and value for money. Within their groups, the farmers maintain records to ensure accountability. The contracts and memorandums of understanding that the groups sign with outside organizations are subject to the law.

Inclusiveness

In the potato project, Excel Hort builds the capacity of growers by helping them form groups and second-tier marketing associations. These sign agreements with other chain actors.

Although the project does not have a special focus on gender, it contributes to the empowerment of women. Women typically grow the potatoes, but the men are in charge of selling the produce, so would usually get the money. But many women now belong to the farmers' groups and sell through the marketing association. That means they, rather than the men, now get the money when the marketing association pays.

Lessons

Even if they have common interests, farmers are used to working as individuals. Their groups do not necessarily function well: they may be inefficient, and it can be hard to manage conflicts. Newly formed groups are still weak and need training on group dynamics. Mistrust and conflict may occur because the marketing associations sell collectively and then divide the revenues among the members according to how much they delivered. To avoid fraud, Excel Hort encourages farmers to open bank accounts with multiple signatories.

Excel Hort wishes to further develop its business models and document the best practices and lessons. It hopes to use this knowledge in other projects, for example through an online platform on agribusiness advisory services.

Getting farmers to work together is important. That lets them mobilize local resources and get outside support – something they cannot do as individuals. It is easier to provide advisory services and technical support to a group. Plus, the group can demand services and make its members' voice heard.

The information boards with urban prices enable farmers to make better decisions about selling produce in Kampala. They are in a better position to bargain, so can get prices for their output.

It is still a challenge to create a system where farmers pay for the services they receive. Farmers are used to getting services for free, so are unwilling to pay for them. Sensitization to help farmers understand the benefits of such services can help, but changing attitudes takes time.

More information

www.excelhort.com

May Murungi, maymurung@gmail.com

5 Cluster B: Subsidized services

Cocoa farmers in Ghana can get loans to buy equipment
Photo: ASI, Ghana

5   Cluster B: Subsidized services

In this cluster, services are largely financed and subsidized by the public sector (governments and donors). Farmers contribute by sharing some of the costs by paying a fee (in cash) or contributing in kind (directly to the service provider) for some of the services.

We describe three examples in this cluster. The farmer training centres in Ethiopia are supported by the government, but farmers also contribute, largely in kind in the form of labour and building materials. In the business service centres in Ghana, smallholders pay for certain services, such as land measurement. Imbaraga is a cooperative in Rwanda that charges its members part of the cost of the services it offers.

Farmer training centres and the IPMS programme in Ethiopia

Marketing farm produce in Ethiopia
Photo: IPMS, Ethiopia

Farmer training centres and the IPMS programme in Ethiopia

Nigatu Alemayehu

When Getachew Seifu faces a problem on his farm, he knows where to go: he heads for the farmer training centre in Hidi, his home village. There he can get all kinds of advice – about what crops and varieties to plant, where to buy seed and chemicals, how to get high yields, and how much various crops are fetching in the market. The centre offers training on a wide range of farming topics. For example, Getachew attended a demonstration about a new variety of tomato, called Kochoro, which has a long shelf life. That means that he does not have to sell immediately at harvest, so can negotiate a better price. And he has doubled his tomato yield to 30 t/ha by using improved techniques.

Figure 35 **The farmer training centres provide information on new farming techniques, improved seed and training on business management**

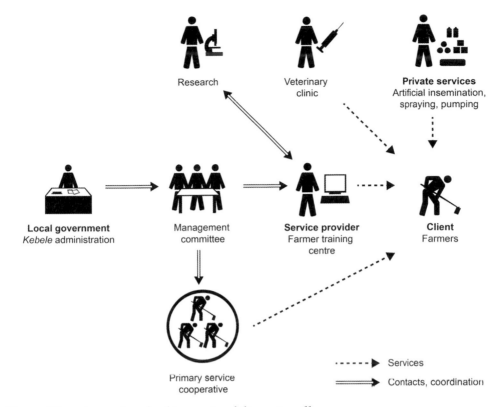

Research Veterinary clinic **Private services** Artificial insemination, spraying, pumping

Local government *Kebele* administration Management committee **Service provider** Farmer training centre **Client** Farmers

Primary service cooperative

- - - - ▶ Services
══════▶ Contacts, coordination

Figure 36   Actors involved in service delivery in villages

Farmer training centres like the one in Hidi are the cornerstone of Ethiopia's strategy to support small-scale farming as a business. The centres were set up in 2002 in each rural *kebele*, the lowest unit of administration in the country (each *kebele* has around 5,000 people). Each farmer training centre is staffed by three extension agents. There are nearly 8,500 such centres throughout the country – though perhaps understandably for such a new and massive initiative, only about 2,500 are fully functional. The government plans to establish about 15,000 centres in all.

The centres are governed by a management committee of between 7 and 10 extension agents and farmers. The committee is chaired by the *kebele* head, who is also a farmer. At its monthly meetings, this committee plans, manages and evaluates the training and demonstration programme. It also organizes farmers to help in setting up and maintaining the demonstration fields.

The centres provide a wide range services: farmer training and extension services on improved farming techniques (through training courses, exhibits, demonstration farms, field days and farmer-to-farmer extension); market-oriented information and advisory services; meeting and communication facilities; and seed and seedlings of new crops, vegetables, fruit and forage varieties. The Ministry of Agriculture has developed some 20 training modules for use in the centres.

The centres are part of a system of agricultural services in each *kebele* (Figure 36). The primary service cooperative supplies inputs. A public animal-health clinic offers veterinary services. Private providers do artificial insemination, treat livestock, spray crops, and rent out water pumps. Innovative farmers organize their own field days. The training centres are also linked to research centres in each Zone in Ethiopia.

Many of these services complement what the training centres do. Relations with them tend to be informal, though the training centres' management committees are increasingly coordinating their work. The use of farmer-to-farmer services is increasing, also with coordination by the committees.

Overcoming limitations: The IPMS project

Unfortunately the government budget is tight, so after paying for staff salaries, there is very little money left for regular activities. That limits the types of work that the training centres can undertake. So in practice, many of the functions listed above depend on projects funded by the government, donors or NGOs, that use the centre facilities and take advantage of their staff for training, management and facilitation.

A 5-year (2004–10) project known as **Improving Productivity and Market Success of Ethiopian Farmers** (IPMS for short) aimed to overcome some of these problems. This project was funded by the Canadian International Development Agency (CIDA) and implemented by the International Livestock Research Institute (ILRI) on behalf of the Ethiopian Ministry of Agriculture.

IPMS focused on 40 pilot farmer training centres. It invested small amounts (around 10%) of the costs of investment and running the centres to leverage their contributions and facilitate market-led, knowledge-based transformation. It provided on-the-job training to extension staff, linked the centres with research institutions, provided market information, and put farmers in touch with input suppliers and produce markets. It provided motorbikes and paid for fuel so the extension agents could reach farmers. It offered short courses for farmers, organized field days, and encouraged both extension agents and farmers by giving prizes for performance.

It also established knowledge centres at the *woreda* level (the next level of local administration above the *kebele*), with printed materials and electronic access to a wide range of information and training materials on markets, production technologies, input suppliers, as well as the latest updates, news and unbiased opinion. It set up similar but smaller information units in each *kebele* centre.

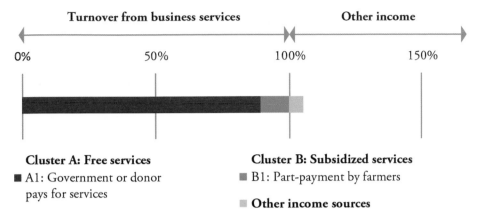

Figure 37   Share of business models in the farmer training centres' revenue

Business models

The farmer training centres are financially supported by the government, and by projects such as IPMS. Farmers also cover some of the costs.

Business model B1: Part-payment by farmers

Farmers contribute significantly to the centres in two ways. First, they have helped build them by providing labour and some of the construction materials. This is equivalent to nearly 40% of the total investment costs of a centre (the rest was paid by the government and the IPMS project), and about 10% of a centre's business-service turnover. The second way that farmers contribute is by volunteers working on the centres' demonstration fields.

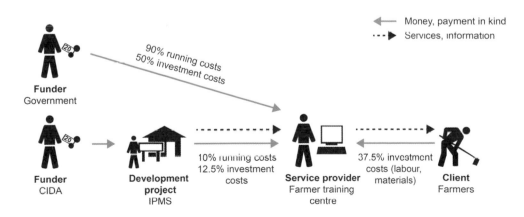

Figure 38   The farmer training centres' business model B1

Business model A1: Government or donor pays for services to farmers

The most common business model is still the provision of free services to farmers. This represents about 90% of the centre's turnover.

Other sources of income

The centres sell the produce from the demonstration fields, generating further income.

Results

Demand for the centres' services is high. Farmers have adopted a number of other new production techniques, such as new cereal and potato varieties, legume varieties, and vegetable production, as well as bio-fertilizers for pulse growing, and urea-molasses as cattle feed. They have started selling their grain and vegetables on the basis of weight rather than by the number of bags or boxes. They have been able to decide where and when to sell their produce on the basis of price information they received through the centres.

Extension workers (called "development agents" in Ethiopia) provide marketing information on the centres' billboards, and update this every week. The marketing committee, an ad-hoc committee of farmers, visits markets in other areas (or contacts them by phone) to check on commodity prices and availability. The market information system is not yet perfect. The information provided by the training centres is general, and does not focus on particular crops that they are promoting. And some information is not yet available: the price of hot peppers (an important local commodity), for example, is determined in Addis Ababa, and is not provided to the farmers.

Accountability

The centre's management committee is key to ensuring the centre is accountable to its clients. It bases its plans and activities on the perceived priorities of local farmers. Issues such as gender and HIV/AIDS are also taken into account. The committee reports to the district office of agriculture about the training centre's work and any serious issues that may arise. Such issues can also be raised in meetings of the village general assembly.

While it was operating, IPMS monitored how satisfied the farmers were with the extension service and the training centres. In addition, district extension staff assess farmers' demands and report these to the district office of agriculture for consideration in planning the next phase of the project.

During field days and training centre meetings, farmers are invited to reflect on what they have learned and any improvements needed. The farmers are not directly involved in assessing the performance of the extension agents, but do so indirectly through the management committee and the field days.

Sustainability

The farmer training centres provide many of their services for free. They get their funding from four sources: the government, donor-funded projects, the sale of products, and the local community.

The bulk of the funding for the centres comes from the regional governmental Bureau of Agriculture (part of the Ministry of Agriculture and Rural Development). This covers investment costs, staff salaries, fuel and allowances. But there is no budget to run the centres' extension activities. Donor-funded projects such as IPMS support the centres in various ways: they contribute information materials and equipment, training, facilitation and some running costs. The centres earn some money by selling produce from demonstration plots, as well as honey, coffee, and seed and seedlings. This revenue is supposed to pay for running costs: things like electricity, internet subscriptions and security. Local people provide materials such as stones, sand and timber, as well as labour to construct the centre buildings. They also help plough, plant weed and harvest the demonstration-farm plots.

The government hopes that the centres will be able to cover more of their costs from the sale of products (Box 8). For some training centres, sales from the demonstration farm are the main income, but this is not the case for Hidi *kebele*, which got top-up funding from the IPMS programme.

Inclusiveness

All the farmers in the *kebele* have the same opportunity to take part in training centre's activities and organized events such as demonstrations, technology exhibitions, field days

---

Box 8   Atsibi *woreda*, Tigray: A sustainable farmer training centre

In the farmer training centre in Atsibi *woreda*, Tigray, the extension agent runs the demonstration farm like a business. It sells improved breeds of sheep, beehives and chicks to farmers, and fruit, vegetables, and milk to the local markets. It uses the revenues to pay for its extension and training activities. It has managed to develop its training facilities. Local farmers donated labour, stones and building materials to construct the facilities and run the demonstration farm.

The highly entrepreneurial extensionist started off by buying a low-cost drip-irrigation system for 950 birr. He planted tomatoes, repaid the loan, took a bigger loan to buy a cow, and began diversifying into new horticultural crops. He reinvested the profits in the training centre; that led to more demonstrations and a sophisticated water-harvesting system, as well as purchase of equipment

The Atsibi farmer training centre has become the model in Tigray for demonstrating and training other development agents on how to finance the training centres.

Source: Adapted from IFPRI 2010

---

and meetings. They can also contribute to the centres by helping build facilities and maintain the field demonstrations.

The information on the billboards is broadcast over the village loudspeaker so illiterate people can also get the information. Classroom training, however, is open only to literate villagers.

Women are encouraged to participate in the activities. The centres aim for women to be half of the participants in all their activities, but this goal is seldom achieved. The centres occasionally hold special field days for women on subjects like vegetable production.

Challenges

Budget constraints. Various efforts, funded by the government, donors and NGOs, aim to improve both the training centres' programmes and their ability to generate their own income. Their ability to do so depends heavily on the abilities of the management committee and the extension agents.

Delivery of services. Illiteracy among farmers, and limited funding and staff skills constrain the centres' ability to deliver training and other services. The centres try to complement their training courses with practice-oriented activities such as demonstration sites, field days and exhibitions.

Staff turnover. The rapid turnover of extension agents hampers the development of strong relations between the centres and the community. Many development agents are rapidly transferred or promoted, while others leave the service to work with NGOs or private companies.

Administrative interference. *Woreda* administrations often interfere in training-centre matters, for example, by ordering the staff to call farmers for meetings. Tired of such events, the farmers often decline invitations to other types of meetings too. Such duties also cut the time that staff have to support the farmers. The local administration should use other channels to reach its constituents.

Relations with other service providers. Links between the training centres and other service providers (notably cooperatives, private enterprises and research agencies, larger-scale farmers) and actors such as commercial farms, still require improvement. The management committees can also coordinate better with the innovative farmers who are involved in farmer-to-farmer extension.

Market orientation. The new Agricultural Growth Programme, funded by donors and the government, aims to further develop the centres, notably in agribusiness development and market information. This programme foresees the construction of a market warehouse in the village, as well as market-oriented training. The village loudspeaker could be used to broadcast market information.

Lessons

The farmer training centres are the most accessible and affordable source of business development services in the *kebele*. This is because the extension agents are stationed in the villages, and they know the people. There is no need to deploy expensive consultants or pay their transport costs. Because the activities are held in the village, they are convenient for farmers to attend, and they do not incur travel expenses. Investing in the training centres is an important and effective contribution to building the capacities and skills of farmers and increasing their food and income security.

The sustainability of the training centres and their services requires adequate financial support from the government and development agencies. The centres will also have to generate their own income, persuade local people to support them with voluntary work, and encourage innovative farmers to continue the farmer-to-farmer extension programmes. That is a complex balancing act.

More information

IFPRI. 2010. In-depth assessment of the public agricultural extension system of Ethiopia and recommendations for improvement. IFPRI discussion paper 01041, December 2010, eastern and southern Africa regional office. International Food Policy Research Institute.

www.ipms-ethiopia.org

Nigatu Alemayehu, n.alemayehu@cgiar.org

Business service centres
for cocoa in Ghana

Farmers queuing to deposit money in their savings
accounts with a mobile banking van at the farmers'
business service centre in Sefwi Wiawso
Photo: ASI, Ghana

Business service centres for cocoa in Ghana

Prince Dodoo

For the last few years, Ghanaian cocoa-growers have been able to get a combination of advice, inputs and credit from farmers' business service centres. There are two such centres: one in Sefwi Wiawso in the Western Region, and a second in New Edubiase, in the Ashanti Region. These centres have been set up with support from Agribusiness Systems International (ASI) as part of the Cocoa Livelihoods Programme, a $40 million multi-country initiative to improve the livelihoods of 200,000 cocoa farmers in West Africa. Beginning in 2009, this programme is managed by the World Cocoa Foundation and funded by 14 big chocolate companies and the Bill and Melinda Gates Foundation. It is implemented jointly by a large number of organizations.

Along with the Cocoa Livelihoods Programme, private-sector input dealers are an important source of finance for the business centres' activities. The dealers are interested in supporting the centres because they can thereby expand their customer base. The centres also operate a credit programme: groups of farmers can approach a local microfinance organization, Opportunity International Savings & Loans, for a loan to cover the cost of inputs.

Each business centre has a manager and four staff: an extension agent, an input salesperson, and two community facilitators. They provide two kinds of services to farmers: free of charge (about 65% of the services provided), and fee-based, where farmers have to pay. The free services develop the farmers' capacities; the fee-based ones help them make productive investments.

Business models

The centres operate three types of business models.

Business model B1: Part-payment by farmers

Many farmers do not know how large their farms are, so do not know how much fertilizer and other chemicals to buy, or how many labourers to hire. The business service centres have obtained the services of three US Peace Corps volunteers to use global positioning systems to measure the farms. Their main task will be to produce maps of 1,000 pilot

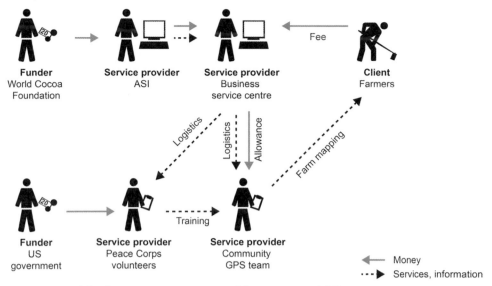

Funder
World Cocoa
Foundation

Service provider
ASI

Service provider
Business
service centre

Client
Farmers

Fee

Logistics

Logistics

Allowance

Farm mapping

Funder
US
government

Service provider
Peace Corps
volunteers

Service provider
Community
GPS team

Training

Money

Services, information

Figure 39   The business service centres' business model B1

farms, and to train a team attached to the business centres how to do this. Farmers pay a share of these services, which account for around 30% of the centres' revenue.

Business model A1: Government or donor pays for services to farmers

This model accounts for about half the centres' revenue. Services offered include:

Extension and business advisory services. The staff offer advice to farmers on a wide range of subjects – not just cocoa. They can provide information on crops, pests and diseases and farm business advice. In a 16-month period in 2011 and 2012, over 3,500 farmers came into the two centres seeking such advice. About one-third of these visitors were women. Many farmers use their mobile phones to call the centres with queries.

Market and research information. The centres act as a link between relevant research institutions and farmers by distributing farmer-friendly leaflets and brochures on a range of topics. The centres also distribute magazines and newspapers of interest to the farmers.

Community outreach and radio programmes. The centre staff visit individual farmers or groups in the villages to understand their needs and identify constraints. They introduce the centre to the farmers and encourage them to form groups so they can take advantage of its services. The centres also organize a weekly radio programme about cocoa farming practices. The shows offer technical advice, give business tips and answer questions that listeners phone in.

Figure 40   The business service centres' business model A1

Training. The centres arrange for two other partners in the Cocoa Livelihoods Programme, the Ghana Cocoa Board (the government agency in charge of the national cocoa industry) and GIZ (a German development agency) to train groups of farmers on farming practices and business management. This training is a requirement for farmers who wish to take advantage of the centres' input credit programme. The centres also collaborate with volunteer programmes (such as one run by ACDI/VOCA) to train farmers in group dynamics and management. These programmes have enabled the centres also to train farmers on other crops, such as maize and rice, and on postharvest technology. In the second quarter of 2012, 400 non-cocoa farmers were trained.

Assistance with financial services. During the community outreach work, the centre staff encourage farmers to open accounts with Opportunity International Savings & Loans. A centre staff member accompanies the Opportunity International personnel to the villages and helps farmers open group and personal savings accounts. The business centre in Sefwi Wiawso has given the microfinance organization temporary office space in its premises. Farmers can also go to a mobile banking van outside the centre to deposit or withdraw money.

> ### Business model C2: Embedded services

Fertilizers in Ghana are heavily subsidized by the government. That means they are cheap. But it also means they can be scarce. Fortunately, the business centres have managed to sign an agreement with the Ghana Cocoa Board that names them as a major distribution agent for the fertilizer. In 2011, the centres purchased 5,000 bags (50 kg) of fertilizer to sell all year round and for use in its input credit programme. In 2012 they tripled their purchase, to 15,000 bags.

The business centres are officially NGOs, so do not wish to sell fertilizers themselves. So they have partnered with a private input dealer, B. Kaakyire Agro Chemicals Ltd., to sell the fertilizer. The dealer pays part of its margin to the business centre. B. Kaakyire also sells a range of other agrochemicals and other farm inputs. The relationship with B. Kaakyire is important for the centres. The input dealer's commercial orientation allows the business centre to become financially sustainable.

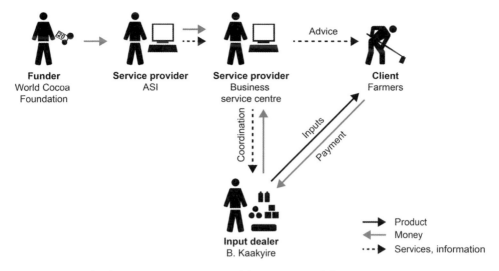

Figure 41   The business service centres' business model C2

A problem with this arrangement was that the farmers could not afford the fertilizer, and local banks are apprehensive about loaning money to farmers. So the centres have developed a service package to make it easy for cocoa farmers to get credit through Opportunity International. The farmers apply for a loan as a group, and the centre staff help them select the inputs they need. The centre forwards their request to Opportunity International, which pays B. Kaakyire to supply the items. The farmers have to start repaying the loan with interest after a 5–6 month grace period. Repayment rates have been 100%: an impressive record. Of the fertilizer received by the centres, 56% has been distributed through this scheme to 980 recipient farmers (about one-third of them women) since the start of the programme.

Embedded services account for around 20% of the centres' revenue.

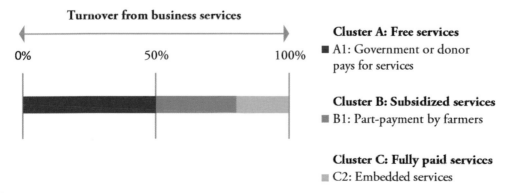

Figure 42   Share of business models in the business service centres' revenue

Results

The centres have had a considerable impact in the 18 months since they were launched.

- Over 1,400 farmers now have bank accounts where they can save money.

- Over 3,500 farmers have accessed extension, market information and farm business advisory services on cocoa and non-cocoa crops.

- The input credit scheme has served 980 farmers in 45 communities, with a total loan portfolio of $493,000. Loans range from $150 to $550, and average of $250 (GH¢ 500). The next input cycle (in 2013) is expected to serve over 2,500 farmers.

- Other banks and agrochemicals companies have seen the success of the input credit scheme, and are getting interested in lending to farmers through similar models.

- Some 400 maize and rice farmers have been trained on good agricultural practices and postharvest technologies.

Sustainability

Margins from sales and user fees. By the end of the Cocoa Livelihoods Programme, it is expected that the business centres will have generated enough funds from the sale of fertilizers and other fee-based services to sustain their operations. This fund will be held in an account which will be made available to the private partner and collaborators and to run the business centres after the project funding ceases.

Strategic partnerships. The business centres have been anchored on a strategic private partner, the input company, B. Kaakyire. The company built an office and a warehouse for the centres and it pays some operational costs. It has indicated a willingness to open other, similar centres elsewhere in Ghana to offer sustainable, demand-driven services for farmers. The Ministry of Food and Agriculture and other government organizations also support the centres. The ministry provides two extension agents at each site to advise farmers. The district- and community-level extension agents of the Ghana Cocoa Board also provide support. Their linkages to both private and governmental organizations are essential to ensure the centres' long-term sustainability, as they are likely to remain in place when donor support comes to an end. The involvement of these strategic partners from the beginning is a key part of the project's design and exit strategy.

Farmer buy-in of services. Farmer groups in the communities around the two centres are very happy with this kind of flexible arrangement. Their commitment is reflected in the excellent repayment rates of 100% for the input credit programme. The fee-based services coupled with sensitization are getting farmers used to the idea that services are not always for free – and that paid-for services are useful.

Inclusiveness

The business service centres are open to both cocoa and non-cocoa farmers, men and women, and large- and small-scale farmers. But they impose criteria. For example, to qualify for the input credit programme, farmers' groups must attend training on good agricultural practices and farm business. The target group is men and women smallholder cocoa farmers who have 1–3 acres (up to a little more than a hectare) of cocoa trees, and who demonstrate an interest in the programme after community sensitization. Plus, borrowers must have a savings account with the microfinance institution, and must deposit 10% of the value of inputs they request into a group account as collateral for the group loan.

Many of the beneficiaries are elderly: there are few young people. The Cocoa Livelihoods Programme targets youth by offering business training. One-quarter of the beneficiaries are women – a respectable figure given that there are no special policies favouring women. To reach more women, the business centres will make their criteria more flexible, offer special credit products and services, and organize events to make it easy for them to attend.

Accountability

The business centres are accountable to the farmers' groups through the group leaders and the centres' community facilitators. The strategy is to disclose fully all information and criteria for each service – especially those services that farmers have to pay for. The service providers at the centres tell the farmers what they have to do to get a service. The centres encourage their clients to tell them if they have any complaints.

The Ghana Cocoa Board ensures that the input credit scheme supplies only approved fertilizers and chemicals. This is checked through field monitoring. The business centre staff facilitate and coordinate the credit programme and ensure that no unapproved chemicals are supplied to the cocoa farmers. They use the centres' monitoring and evaluation system and community outreach visits to check the quality of services provided to farmers. Such visits create trust, feedback and build relationship between the credit provider and farmers – something that was lacking in failed models in the past.

At the programme level, the Cocoa Livelihoods Programme periodically checks how the centres are operating. It does this through focus groups with farmers to get their feedback on the services provided by the centres.

Challenges and lessons

Weakness of the public sector. The public sector is unable to offer efficient and effective support services for agriculture. The extension services have limited capacity, and there are inadequate resources needed to reach farmers.

Functions of the business centres. If business centres are to provide training directly, they will need appropriate training materials and effective ways to engage with farmers. They also need to stimulate demand for their advice, in particular farm business management.

Credit. Tailored loan services need to be combined with training and organization to ensure that farmers are creditworthy. Farmers should initially be given small loans for specific needs, which they can repay easily. Once they demonstrate their ability to repay, they graduate to a larger loan.

Business approach. It is not easy to shift from free (or heavily subsidized) services to commercial provision by the private sector. It sounds obvious, but the business service centres must themselves operate under a business approach. They must develop services that farmers want and are prepared to pay for. Providing services (including credit) to groups rather than individuals is an effective and efficient way of operating. However, the centres retain developmental objectives, and these may conflict with their commercial aims.

Partnerships for sustainability. The business centres are an example of how a limited-term project can leverage resources and give the public and private sectors incentives to provide services directly. Alone, the input dealers, banks and extension services have inadequate expertise, time and ability to coordinate their activities. The Cocoa Livelihoods Programme has created an institution, the business service centre, in which partners can collaborate for the benefit of their rural clients.

More information

www.asintl.org/ourexperience-cocoa-livelihoods-program.html

Prince Dodoo, pdodoo@acdivocaghana.org

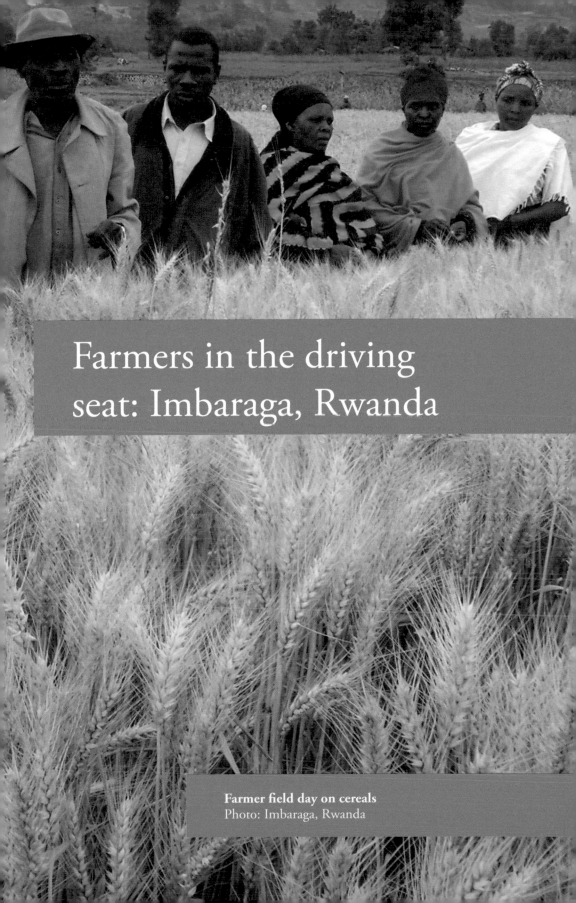

Farmers in the driving seat: Imbaraga, Rwanda

Farmer field day on cereals
Photo: Imbaraga, Rwanda

Farmers in the driving seat: Imbaraga, Rwanda

J. Richard N. Kanyarukiga and Joseph Gafaranga

Imbaraga is a farmers' federation established in March 1992 in Kigali, Rwanda. An apex organization that represents all farmers in Rwanda, Imbaraga was founded to unite farmers so they could gain a collective voice for lobbying and advocacy. At the start, Imbaraga's membership was 3,000. It has gradually increased to almost 95,000 in 2011. Six out of ten members are small-scale farmers who cultivate no more than 0.5 hectares. Almost all the rest (37%) have 0.5 to 2 hectares; only 3% have more. The members are associated either into informal groups of 25–30 households or into cooperatives with 10–80 members.

Imbaraga has its headquarters in Kigali, the capital, and is present in all four of the country's rural provinces. The branch in Northern Province, operating from Musanze district, is generally considered the pioneer and leader. It has about 20,000 members, organized in 100 cooperatives, and a permanent staff of 22. The annual membership fee is RwF 1,000 per person (about $1.60).

Imbaraga's main aim is to support farmers to become successful entrepreneurs who are capable of sustaining their families and overcoming the challenges they face in farming. It engages in four main types of activities:

- **Lobbying and advocacy** on policy issues related to land rights and entitlements and commodity prices.

- **Selling inputs and equipment to farmers.** Imbaraga purchases in bulk from major suppliers and resells to input dealers, who in turn sell the inputs to farmers.

- **Providing extension and advisory services.** Imbaraga runs training programmes at its training facility at Cyuve (Northern Province), through farmer field schools, and by organizing farmer visits. The organization's team of agronomists do most of the training and provide extension services; outside specialists give specialized training on subjects such as processing.

- **Marketing of farmers' produce.** Imbaraga helps its members synchronize the production, management and harvesting of crops, sets up collection centres, and organizes the processing and packaging of the crops for delivery to large buyers.

Lobbying and advocacy

Imbaraga's main activity is lobbying and advocacy for farmers' concerns in national policy-making. An example is its initiative to improve the functioning of food markets. Prices of farm produce in Rwanda vary markedly from month to month. The resulting uncertainty discourages farmers from producing. To address this issue, in 2010 Imbaraga engaged local governments, traders and the Ministry of Agriculture in consultations. The stakeholders agreed on a price range, setting the minimum and maximum prices at which crops were to be traded. Imbaraga bought all the produce through its collection centres, and traders bought from Imbaraga rather than from individual farmers. With markets stable, farmers are now stepping up production.

Sale of inputs and equipment

Imbaraga mobilizes farmers to buy inputs from authorized providers, and it resells quality seed, fertilizers, equipment and other inputs to farmers. It contracts local artisans to make a range of simple equipment for sale to farmers. It also supplies items such as power tillers for ploughing and haulage, hand-held and pedal-driven maize hullers, drying sheds, packaging materials, and grading racks and wash sinks for potatoes. All technologies are specially designed for small-scale farmers.

Figure 43   Imbaraga lobbies various arms of the government to promote the interests of farmers

Extension and advisory services

Imbaraga helps farmers increase their productivity by training them in farming methods, processing, entrepreneurship and marketing techniques. It helps them to strengthen their organizations, obtain land titles, and promotes gender issues, democracy and governance.

Imbaraga provides training in improved postharvest handling and storage. That enables farmers to meet the quality standards of major buyers such as the Ministry of Agriculture, the Rwanda Agriculture Board and the Strategic Grain Reserve. These buyers offer higher prices: for instance in 2011–12, the farm-gate price for maize averaged RwF 150/kg, while the Ministry and Agriculture Board paid RwF 260/kg.

Marketing

Imbaraga buys produce from its members, bulks it and sells it to major buyers. It deals mainly in maize, wheat and beans. Farmers may also opt, through their cooperatives, to sell their produce to other buyers.

Business models

Imbaraga's provincial organizations are semi-autonomous, and can develop business models suited to their own areas. The Northern Province branch of Imbaraga has the following models:

Business model B2: Subsidized cooperative services for members

The services Imbaraga delivers to its own members are partly financed by the membership fees that Imbaraga collects. The services include training, study tours and market linkages. The trainees may be representatives of the groups or cooperatives, or individual farmer members. This model accounts for about one-third of the revenue of Imbaraga's Northern Province branch.

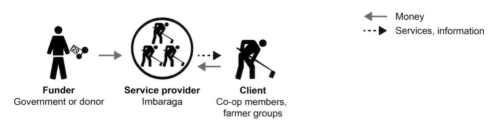

Funder	**Service provider**	**Client**
Government or donor	Imbaraga	Co-op members, farmer groups

←— Money
···▶ Services, information

Figure 44   Imbaraga's business model B2

Business model A1: Government or donor pays for services to farmers

A donor (the government, an international agency or NGO) pays Imbaraga for delivering services to its member cooperatives and farmer groups. These may then pass on these services to their individual member farmers. Imbaraga also provides certain services directly to farmers, without going through the intermediate organization. The services include training on improved production techniques, record-keeping and storage, market facilitation and linkages, advocacy, and access to credit. This model accounts for about two-thirds of the revenue of Imbaraga's Northern Province branch.

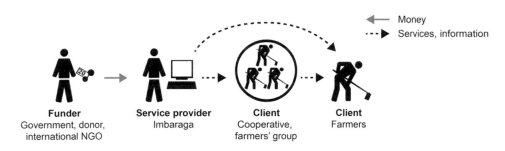

Figure 45   **Imbaraga's business model A1**

Business model C1: Services paid by the client

Imbaraga's third-most important model is delivering services to a client in return for a fee. One of these services is training: Imbaraga is certified to deliver training that agricultural dealers are obliged to pass. Trainees have to pay a fee (about $8 each) for the course. The course focuses mainly on input use, storage management and marketing.

Imbaraga also provides market-linkage services directly to larger farmers who are not members. Imbaraga charges a fee for this.

Other sources of income

Imbaraga has various other sources of income, accounting for about 40% of its total income. It buys maize, wheat and beans from farmers (including large farmers who are not members), bulks the product, and sells it to large buyers like the World Food Programme, big traders, the Rwanda Agricultural Board and the Strategic Grain Reserve.

Imbaraga also sells various types of equipment specifically adapted for smallholders. It orders these items from local artisans.

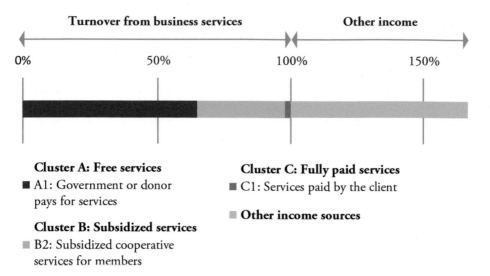

Figure 46 **Share of business models in Imbaraga Northern Province's revenue**

It also generates income by renting out its training facilities (conference hall, accommodation, catering, etc.). It sometimes hosts or co-organizes training programmes for various clients.

Imbaraga is looking into the option to become a commissioned agent of the Equity Bank (Rwanda) Ltd. This could facilitate its members and non-members' access to financial services such as savings, credit and investment advice from the bank. Equity Bank will pay it a commission for this service.

Results

Thanks to Imbaraga, farmers in Northern Province have learned new production techniques and postharvest handling and storage methods. Potato productivity, for instance, has been raised from an average of 12 tons of potatoes to 20 tons per hectare. Likewise, productivity of maize and wheat has grown from an average of 500 kg to 4–5 tons per hectare. For climbing beans, productivity has risen from 800 kg to 2.5–3.5 tons per hectare. Farmers say this is thanks to Imbaraga's training, a guaranteed supply of inputs, collective marketing, and access to markets via Imbaraga's collection centres.

The farmers have seen their livelihoods improve as a result. Educational levels and enrolment in health insurance schemes have gone up, and more are now not only self-sufficient in food production, but have also improved their houses. Many have climbed out of poverty.

Sustainability

Imbaraga has been increasingly successful in generating funds and diversifying its sources of income. It gets its funding from members' annual contributions, fees for services, support from the Rwandan government, and finance from a number of regional and international partners. Imbaraga is 100% owned by its farmer members, who have an interest in maintaining it. Members' contributions amount to RwF 7 million, or nearly 10% of this total turnover (in 2010–11 RwF 72 million, or $115,000).

Inclusiveness

All members of Imbaraga are small-scale farmers. Imbaraga helps them to organize themselves to strengthen their bargaining power. It has an active women's programme to ensure that women are represented up to the national level, and has a special youth programme. Imbaraga also gives direct support to vulnerable groups – including aid in house-building and the free delivery of seed, fertilizer and other inputs.

Accountability

Imbaraga is answerable to its farmer members (who are its owners): they elect Imbaraga's office bearers at the national, regional and district levels. All members constitute the annual general assembly, which also forms the electoral body. Members' representatives take part in planning, implementing, monitoring and evaluating activities. An annual audit is held by a commissioned external auditor. In March 2012, the Office of the Ombudsman highly commended Imbaraga for its good governance and community empowerment.

Challenges

Despite its successes, Imbaraga still faces many challenges. Illiteracy hampers its training programmes. Farmers who cultivate less than a hectare have little room to experiment and innovate. Poor infrastructure (roads, electricity and market information) hinder market access. Big fluctuations in market prices, and the high prices of farm inputs (particularly seed and fertilizers) make it difficult for farmers to plan and to make a profit. Variable weather damages crops and cuts yields.

Most of these constraints are out of Imbaraga's control, and the organization has limited financial and human resources to intervene where it is needed most. In response, it has intensified its income-generation activities, stepping up its contacts with existing and new donors.

Lessons

Imbaraga acknowledges that ownership by its members is a key to all its achievements. It has proven that farmers' organizations can help their members generate sustainable incomes. It does this by providing appropriate training and ensuring consistent and affordable access to good inputs and markets.

Conducive government policy and responsive community mobilization have been key factors underlying the organization's success.

Imbaraga maintains its commitment to helping its members access lucrative markets and develop an attitude of competitive entrepreneurship. It is exploring new ways of sharing information, such as through a website (www.umuhinzi.com) and through magazines such as *Amajyambere* ("Development").

More information

www.imbaraga.org

J. Richard N. Kanyarukiga, jrnkanyarukiga@yahoo.com
Joseph Gafaranga, gafarangajo@yahoo.fr

6 Cluster C:
Fully paid services

Processors want to buy in bulk – and that means organizing smallholder farmers
Photo: DADTCO, Mozambique

6   Cluster C: Fully paid services

Under this cluster, services are fully paid by the client. We include two examples of embedded services, both in Mozambique: Bindzu's input supply and other services, and DADTCO's cassava-purchasing scheme. We have two examples where clients pay the full costs of the services they receive: ESDC in Uganda, and Target in Ethiopia.

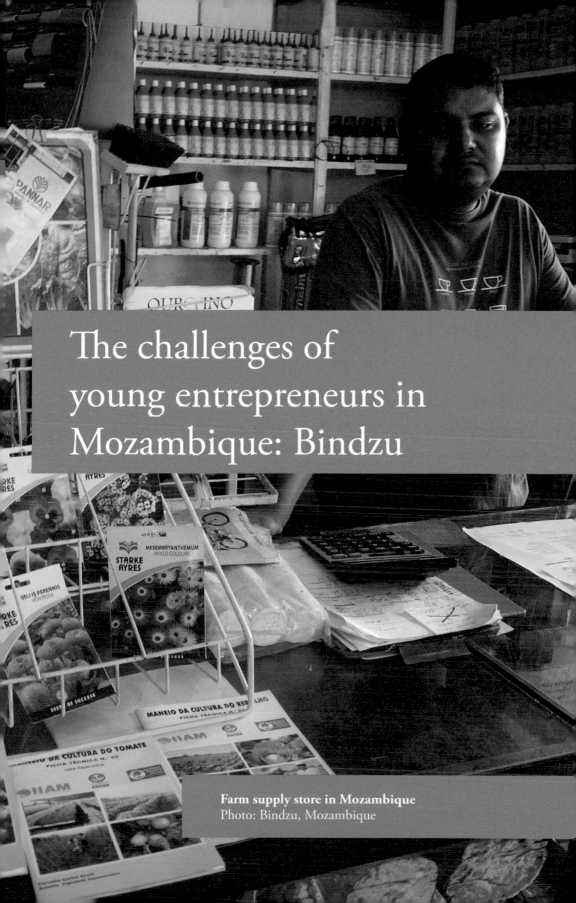

The challenges of young entrepreneurs in Mozambique: Bindzu

Farm supply store in Mozambique
Photo: Bindzu, Mozambique

The challenges of young entrepreneurs in Mozambique: Bindzu

Márcia Maposse

T he 400 or so members of the Bloco 1 and 2 Farmer Associations in Moamba had been producing green beans for several years. But they could never be sure what price they would get when they came to sell.

There were two reasons for this. First, the market price fluctuated wildly – from a low of $0.15 per kilogram in the peak season, up to $6 when the beans were scarce. Second, the quality of the farmers' output also varied: customers who wanted uniform high quality turned up their noses if the farmers delivered crates of uneven beans.

The Mozambican Institute for Export Promotion (IPEX) came to help the farmers improve their production and marketing. At first it hired a consultant to plant and manage a half-hectare demonstration plot in the area. But the local people did not know the person they hired: they wanted someone who worked with them every day, in the field. So they suggested that IPEX contact Bindzu, a local agribusiness firm.

That worked out better. A Bindzu staff member visited the farmers regularly for about 6 months, advising them on how to plant seed, apply fertilizers, and irrigate the beans. The farmers were impressed by his knowledge.

Bindzu (which means "production" in Changana, the local language) started in 2010 by four university students with funds from ADIPSA (a Danish-funded programme that supports private sector initiatives), a commercial bank and the local government. When Bindzu started work, the local farmers were sceptical. Farmers in Mozambique tend to be poor and old: what were these young, urban people up to, growing crops? But the neighbours were curious and came to visit, and came away impressed by the techniques the young people were using, and by their knowledge and ideas.

That was a wake-up call for Bindzu. The owners realized that to improve their output, local farmers needed two things: inputs and advice. Inputs such as fertilizer, chemicals and equipment were sold at prices much higher than across the border in neighbouring South Africa. And information about improved technologies was also hard to find. Bindzu saw a market opportunity.

ADIPSA had hired Bindzu to help some other young professionals develop their business plans. With the income from these consultancies and its first vegetable harvests, Bindzu set up a shop in Moamba, a town midway between Maputo and the South African border. This sells farm inputs and supplies, and provides free advice to farmers who buy there. It also is a convenient meeting-point for farmers, allowing Bindzu staff to listen to their needs and interests. That has led Bindzu to broaden its range of products and services: it now ploughs land for farmers, and sells irrigation systems and seedlings. It also helps individuals and farmer groups prepare business plans. It charges a reduced fee for this service, on the understanding that if the plans are successful, the farmers will pay the remainder of the fee and will come back to Bindzu to buy the inputs they need.

Results

By 2011, the company's turnover had grown to $200,000. It re-invested what it could: it bought a new lorry and some more land, expanded the shop, and diversified its product range. The idea is to turn the shop into a "one-stop shop" for farmers, where they can get inputs, tractor services and advice – as well as sell their produce. Bindzu currently has a staff of 14 permanent staff, and employs a variable number of seasonal workers for harvesting and sowing.

Bindzu provides a range of services through the various models:

- **Inputs.** At the centre is the company's shop in Moamba. Bindzu benefits from its linkages with Omnia, an input supplier in South Africa, from which it buys products at a reduced price. That enables it to offer lower prices than most other input suppliers in the area.

- **Advice.** Bindzu provides advice (either at the shop or in the farmers' fields, if they are not too far away) on planting, spacing, seed, fertilizers, pesticides, irrigation, etc.

- **Soil-fertility tests.** Bindzu takes soil samples to Omnia's laboratories in South Africa. It sometimes includes this service in the price of the inputs or other services (such as business plans) that the clients buy. It also sells the service as a separate option.

- **Land preparation for planting.** Bindzu owns three tractors, bought through a loan from CEPAGRI, a government body that promotes agriculture. The services are charged per hour. They are in high demand, and the company expects to have repaid the loans it took to buy the tractors within 5 years. It is thinking of expanding these services to other districts, but lack of capital is still a problem.

- **Developing business plans.** As mentioned above, in 2010 Bindzu was contracted by ADIPSA to train eight young farmers and two small agribusinesses to set up horticultural enterprises. In 2011 it helped an association and another three farmers to prepare business plans so they could get credit from a bank. Bindzu charges a percentage of the total investment envisaged in the business plans; the maximum fee is 10%. Large farmers have to pay up front; small farmers pay only part in advance; they pay the rest if the credit is approved.

When Bindzu helps design a business plan, it may follow this up with other services if the client so desires. Bindzu may even supervise the entire production process, from land preparation through planting, fertilization, irrigation, pest control and harvest to commercialization.

Central to all its advisory services is Bindzu's connection with the market. The advice it gives on planting certain crops, for example, depends on the expected price in the market and the time of harvest.

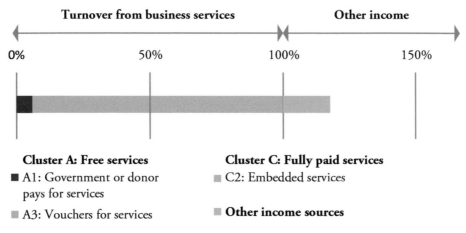

Figure 47   Share of business models in Bindzu's revenue

Business models

Bindzu uses a mix of three business models.

Business model C2: Embedded services

Bindzu's main business model involves the sale of a package of inputs and services to farmers, who pay for it. The embedded services include market information, business plans

Figure 48   Bindzu's business model C2

and technical assistance. This is an important source of revenue for the company: over 80% of its business-service turnover in 2011. Bindzu expects it to remain the company's main business model in the future.

Business model A1: Government or donor pays for services to farmers

Bindzu also operate the free service model, in which a funder (the government or a donor) contracts Bindzu to provide services to farmers and young professionals. This accounted for more than 5% of the company's business-service turnover in 2011.

Business model A3: Vouchers for services

Another model is the use of vouchers. Farmers request a government fund for production inputs and services. The fund pays Bindzu directly, and gives farmers receipts, which serve as vouchers. They present these at Bindzu in exchange for the products or services they want. This model made up more than 10% of Bindzu's business-service turnover in 2011.

Other sources of income

In addition, the company earns money from activities apart from business services. This works in three ways:

First, Bindzu produces fruit and vegetables itself, often using its own funds or money borrowed from a bank. These sales contribute to 10% of the company's total revenues. Its 3 ha site also serves as a demonstration plot to show techniques to other farmers and potential customers.

Second, Bindzu also operates as a trader, buying produce from farmers and selling it on into the value chain. When buying, Bindzu sometimes gives informal technical advice (when to plant, when to sell, etc.). This accounted for 5% of the company's total turnover in 2011. Though this is still a small percentage, Bindzu hopes it will be an important business model in the future.

Third, in 2012 Bindzu started a partnership with farmers who own land near a sugarcane processing plant. Some of the landowners are involved in production; others are not. The farmers provide the land and labour, while Bindzu provides funding and technical assistance. The profit from this activity will be shared between Bindzu (60%) and the farmers (40%). The company is currently working on 250 hectares under this model. It has high hopes that this will generate sufficient revenues in 2012 to sustain the company.

Sustainability

Bindzu's main sustainability strategy is not to rely on one business model, and to avoid risky operations. It has learned this the hard way: a consignment of poor-quality seed potatoes led to a crop failure. An unreliable greenhouse contractor charged a lot but built little. And Bindzu provided a batch of fertilizer on credit but was not repaid, leaving Bindzu with debt and cash-flow problems. That meant it could not pay Omnia, its wholesale supplier, on time, and the South African firm suspended deliveries. It resumed them only after a representative visited Bindzu and learned the cause of the problems.

As a result, Bindzu has stopped supplying items on credit, and has begun offering a more varied range of services to earn money, such as renting out tractors. This is when it got involved in trading the output of large farmers.

But Bindzu's financial situation remains unstable: Omnia has again decided to stop providing inputs on credit, and it has opened an outlet in Maputo that competes directly with Bindzu's shop in Moamba.

Bindzu is not lying back waiting for its luck to change. It is negotiating with Omnia on which areas it should serve, and which areas Omnia wants to serve directly. Bindzu continues to look for gaps in the market that it can plug, such as producing sugarcane on land near processing plants, and doing consultancy work. It also hopes it can start getting contracts with the government or big international organizations to provide inputs to large-scale programmes.

Inclusiveness

Bindzu clearly states that its clients are not only small farmers, but also larger ones. Nevertheless, around 60% of its clients farm only 0.5–1 ha of land. But they often fail to pay for services (such as ploughing) or inputs, and few request services directly. Bindzu staff have to stimulate demand from this clientele through the company's demonstration plot and by contacting them directly.

When it comes to young entrepreneurs, Bindzu staff makes a point of trying to enthuse young women about getting involved in agribusiness.

Accountability

Bindzu's history shows that the company takes this seriously: it actively seeks new demands and gaps to fill. Sometimes Bindzu gets negative reactions from clients about a service (such as land preparation) that was not done well. The company takes this seriously: it goes back to the farm to do the job properly, at no extra cost.

Challenges

Young professionals need to be persistent if they want to be successful: new companies have ups and downs. The founding partners of Bindzu had to go for long months without salary – not to mention profits! They have had to cope with the personal difficulties and uncertainties this entails.

Bindzu avoids giving inputs on credit to small farmers: they often cannot repay. That endangers the company's financial health. Sometimes farmers cannot repay because market prices have fallen unexpectedly. At other times, they avoid paying because they see Bindzu as a donor rather than a company. This is a big challenge for Bindzu: to make farmers understand that it is a business and needs to be treated as such.

Precisely because farmers are not always able to pay, Bindzu needs to rely on a variety of sources of income. Key to doing this is offering services along the value chain, because the peak demands for each service is different. That allows you to work throughout the year.

The founders feel they still lack essential skills in business management, and need to think more strategically about the company and attract new clients and larger projects, which will demand new skills. They also need to develop technical expertise such as vegetable production in greenhouses and sugarcane production, and skills that will help them work with their clients more efficiently. Examples of the latter are facilitation skills for working with farmers, support for the formation of small farmers' associations, negotiation and procurement.

In the near future Bindzu would like to expand its services, especially to nearby districts where it sees large market potential. Its current services are in considerable demand, so it has many opportunities. Taking advantage of them will require outside investment.

Lessons

Bindzu's founders know from personal experience what it is like to be a young professional starting up a business. They had to work hard to show they were credible. And on the way, they had to do plenty of learning by doing.

Agribusiness in general requires relatively high investments, so good market research is critical to success.

As of 2012, Bindzu has decided to administer each line of business independently. The aim is to better understand which business model produces the best margins.

More information

http://apf-mozambique.ning.com

Márcia Maposse, bindzu.agrobusiness@gmail.com

The Cassava+ project in Mozambique: DADTCO

The Cassava+ project in Mozambique: DADTCO

Isabel Mazive

Cassava is an important staple crop in northern Mozambique. But smallholder farmers find it difficult to grow on a commercial basis: they have to sell or process the roots quickly as they store poorly after harvest, and they must meet the high costs of transport. They can make dried cassava chips or flour, which are easier to store and cost less to transport, but can be hard to sell. How can markets be developed and cassava-growing made profitable?

DADTCO, the Dutch Agricultural Development & Trading Company, founded in 2002, combines private entrepreneurship with a social vision. DADTCO developed a mobile processing unit to process raw cassava into cake. The cake is pure starch, so ferments readily. That makes it great for making beer. DADTCO approached SAB Miller, a big South African brewer and part-owner of Cervejas de Moçambique, the country's largest brewer. As a result, DADCTO signed an agreement to supply Cervejas de Moçambique with cassava cake, which led to the Cassava+ project.

The processing unit is the size of a 40-foot container, and fits on the back of a lorry. That means that it can be parked near the fields where the cassava is grown, avoiding the need to transport the roots a long way. When all the cassava in the area has been processed, it is easy to move the processing unit to another site and start over again.

To make cake, the roots have to be fresh, and individual farmers cannot harvest enough by hand to fill DADTCO's tractor trailer, let alone the processing unit's daily requirement of 40 tons of roots. So it is necessary to organize farmers to ensure a sufficient and regular supply. DADTCO initially employed local people to mobilize the farmers and identify who should harvest when. They organized groups of neighbouring farmers each to harvest a certain amount of roots for pick-up each day. They made sure that the farmers knew the harvesting requirements: the roots have to be between 12 and 18 months old, not too small, and harvested today. Setting up this system and organizing the farmers took some doing.

Through this arrangement DADTCO provides various types of support to farmers:

- **Technical advice** on suitable cassava varieties, production techniques such as weeding and pest control, crop rotations with legumes to maintain soil fertility, and postharvest handling.

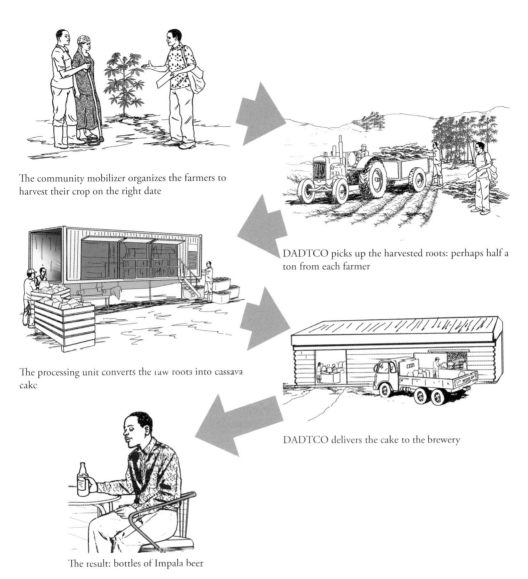

The community mobilizer organizes the farmers to harvest their crop on the right date

DADTCO picks up the harvested roots: perhaps half a ton from each farmer

The processing unit converts the raw roots into cassava cake

DADTCO delivers the cake to the brewery

The result: bottles of Impala beer

Figure 49   How DADTCO turns cassava into beer

- **Provision of new cassava varieties** in partnership with the Mozambican Agriculture Research Institute and Corredor Agro Lda, a private company, which multiplies and distributes the planting materials and trains farmers how to grow them.

- **Organization of farmers** to grow cassava for DADTCO and to harvest on a particular date. This work has been outsourced to the International Fertilizer Development Center (IFDC) with funding from the Dutch government.

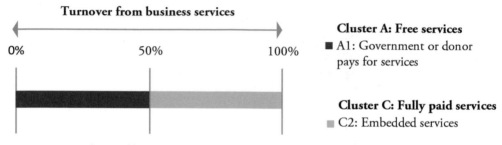

Figure 50   Share of business models in DADTCO's revenue

Results

IFDC has trained 60 "lead farmers" to spearhead the technical extension work. Each one trains at least five of his or her neighbours. The lead farmers grow cassava on a larger scale, and act as hubs for small-scale farmers around them. Inputs are provided either through a voucher programme or by establishing links between the farmers and input dealers.

Between September 2011 and October 2012, DADTCO processed 3,000 tons of cassava into 1,500 tons of cake. It now supplies about 80 tons of cake a week to Cervejas de Moçambique, which uses a mix of 70% cassava cake and 30% malted barley to make Impala-brand beer. This brand is sold mainly in rural areas in Mozambique's three northern provinces. The brewer wants to scale up production and expand into the urban market. It aims for a market share of 10% in Mozambique. This effort is supported by the Mozambican government, which charges only 10% tax on beer made from cassava (compared to a 40% rate on beer based on imported malted barley).

Business model

Business model C2: Embedded services

DADTCO began with a simple business model in which it organized farmers to supply cassava, and bought the roots from them. In this model, the services were embedded in another transaction (buying cassava).

Business model A1: Government or donor pays for services to farmers

As of 2012, the services have been outsourced to IFDC (Figure 52) and are provided for free to farmers. The costs are covered by DADTCO and donors. They will gradually be handed over to the farmer organizations and other users of cassava cake, such as bakeries.

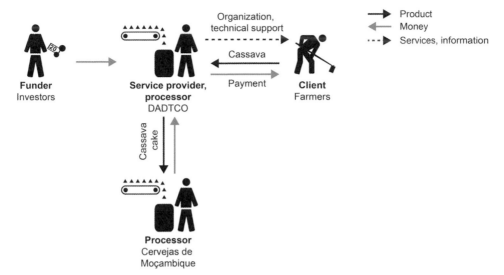

Figure 51   DADTCO's business model C2

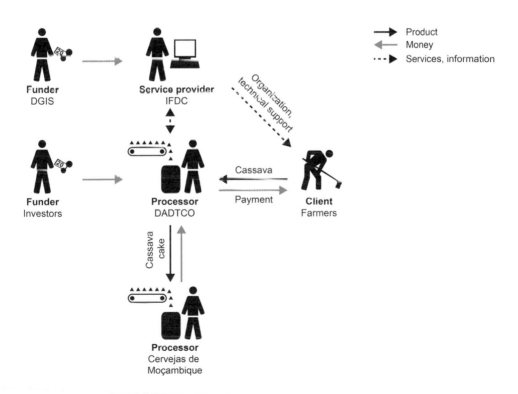

Figure 52   DADTCO's current business model A1

Sustainability

DADTCO now ultimately depends on two organizations: Cervejas de Moçambique (the only current buyer of the cake) and DGIS (the Dutch government donor that supports IFDC's work). DADTCO wants to be less dependent on a single buyer, so it is seeking alternative markets. It has started trials on bread production with a bakery in Nampula, replacing 20% of the flour with cassava cake. Other potential uses of the cake include processed foods, biofuel, animal feed and textiles.

The services that farmers receive are financed partially from the sale of the cake. But DADTCO expects that it cannot fund them fully; they must therefore be financed by donors or by self-organized farmers. The idea is for the lead farmers to take over the role currently performed by IFDC and the community mobilizers. They will pass on technical expertise and new varieties to their neighbours, manage the production of improved, disease-free planting materials, and coordinate their groups to harvest and deliver on schedule.

DADTCO is not yet commercially viable. Losing money in the start-up stages is normal for an investment like this. Its investments have been covered so far by Cervejas de Moçambique – evidence of its faith in DADTCO's ability to supply the inputs it requires.

Inclusiveness

DADTCO's business operations and the services that are tied to it benefit mostly the smallholder farmers in the region. The immediate target is to get 1,500 farmers involved, who will produce 40,000 tons of raw cassava. Special policies (targeted at women, for example) are not part of the project, though possibilities will be explored starting in 2012.

Some questions remain. The lead farmers have larger plots. But how will smaller-scale farmers be affected? And what happens to those who want to sell cassava again next year? As the productivity goes up, the supply of cake may exceed demand from the brewer. Farmers may be left with cassava they cannot sell.

Accountability

The donor will conduct a formal evaluation in October 2012 to assess the project's impact on the farmers' livelihoods and check whether DADTCO's and IFDC's goals are being met. Informally, DADTCO interacts with the farmers when they deliver the cassava to the processing unit. Both the farmers and DADTCO staff take these opportunities to ask questions and get an idea of what is happening.

The "free hand of the market" is also a tool that ensures accountability: if the farmers do not like the services and prices they get, they will not sell their produce to DADTCO. The fact that they are eager to sell their crop to DADTCO indicates that the company and IFDC's services are catering to their needs.

Challenges

The supply of services to farmers depends on the smooth functioning of the **processing unit.** Various things can disrupt this. The supply of cassava roots from the farmers may be interrupted – in which case the processing unit has to stop. Too much cassava may arrive, forcing the unit to work overtime in order to avoid the roots from spoiling. The unit needs to stop work for regular maintenance, and it may break down at other times. Such stoppages force DADTCO to stop buying cassava, disrupting the supply of inputs and depriving the farmers of income. It also interrupts the supply of cake to the brewery. DADTCO maintains a buffer stock of cake (which can be stored longer than the roots) to even out such fluctuations.

Problems with **cassava production** include low yields and inconsistent quality because of a mixture of traditional varieties. That leads to fluctuating beer quality and high maintenance costs at the brewery. By growing modern varieties, farmers could harvest and earn more, and DADTCO would have a more consistent supply of the raw material.

DADTCO is a **processing company**: it has no expertise in farming or community organizing. Its mobilization work was a distraction from its core business.

The **overdependence on one buyer** (Cervejas de Moçambique) is risky: what happens if the brewery stops making Impala, or if it looks elsewhere for supplies? By limiting DADTCO's growth potential, this overdependence restricts the opportunities for large numbers of smallholders. DADTCO is seeking to diversify its markets, for example by finding ways to use cassava cake in bread-making.

The **absence of banks** in in rural Mozambique, and the fact that many farmers are unwilling to open accounts, means that DADTCO has to transport large amounts of money around to pay them in cash. That is risky. DADTCO is considering using Banco Único, a bank that serves small rural businesses, to facilitate payments.

Lessons

Need for organizations with different specializations. When DADTCO started work, the funding for the facilitation work had not yet come through. There were no IFDC field staff to manage this work. So DADTCO had to do it alone, and had to learn how to organize the farmers. Fortunately this worked out well. But in general, it is very important to have people on board at the beginning who have the expertise to organize and train the farmers. This is necessary to avoid delays and inadequate supplies.

Public–private partnerships. This project is based on a new technology: DADTCO's processing unit. This has the potential to transform cassava from a food-security crop to a cash crop. Success so far has been possible because of the linkages between the many actors involved: DADTCO, SABMiller, Cervejas de Moçambique and Corredor Agro in the private sector; the Mozambican and Dutch governments and the research agency in the public sector; and IFDC (an NGO).

Power in the value chain. The brewer is currently the most powerful actor in the value chain. DADTCO currently has no alternative buyers, and the farmers lack the transport and market information they would need to sell their cassava elsewhere. A thorough value chain analysis to look for alternative ways for farmers to reach markets would be welcome.

More information

www.dadtco.nl

Isabel Mazive, i.mazive@dadtco.nl

Serving beekeepers in
Uganda: ESDC

Various designs of beehives in Uganda
Photo: ESDC, Uganda

Serving beekeepers in Uganda: ESDC

Ambrose Bugaari

Honey production is a good source of extra cash for smallholders in Uganda. Yet, beekeepers find it difficult to produce enough honey to meet the demand. Many beekeepers manage their hives poorly, they use outdated techniques and cannot get finance to improve them, and producer groups tend to be weak. They get little government support, partly because policies do not yet regard beekeeping as an agricultural activity.

A business service provider, Effective Skills Development Consultants (ESDC), is working with SNV (a Dutch development agency) and KABECOS (a beekeepers' cooperative) to build beekeepers' skills in Kamwenge district, western Uganda. It is using a "farmer-led"

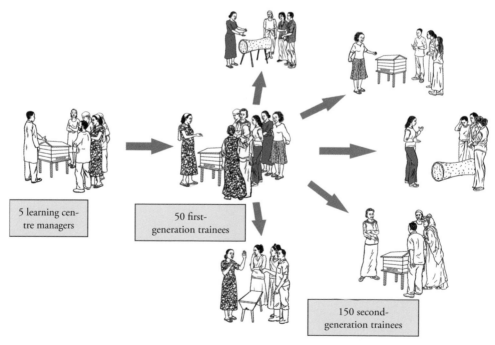

Figure 53   KABECOS uses a farmer-to-farmer training scheme

extension model: one that relies on the beekeepers themselves to spread the skills among the members. It has established five "learning centres", each with at least 20 hives, protective gear, a weighing scale and other equipment. The centre managers were trained by KABECOS. They pass on their skills to 10 beekeepers at their centres. Each of these trainees in turn trains three other beekeepers. The five centres thus reach over 200 beekeepers in all. A big advantage of such a scheme is that once it has been set up, the training does not cost money as the trainers do it on a voluntary basis.

As a result, the beekeepers have increased their output – some by as much as threefold. They have started to process their honey to raise its value. More and more now make candles and other products from the wax, which used to go to waste. They now see beekeeping as a business rather than a hobby. They keep records, and KABECOS has a system to track each person's production. This motivates the farmers to set production targets.

The farmer-led approach is easy to coordinate through the centre managers. The reverse is also true: individual beekeepers can use the same mechanism to reach KABECOS and give feedback about their needs and challenges. Because the trainers also keep bees, it is easy to customize the training to the beekeepers' needs.

Now that the model has been shown to work, KABECOS is planning to expand it to other parts of Kamwenge. SNV and ESDC are already expanding the model in two other districts. The approach also has promise for commodities other than honey.

ESDC: Effective Skills Development Consultants

ESDC (Effective Skills Development Consultants) was a key player in setting up the KABECOS learning centres. Founded in 1999, ESDC is a private company that supports enterprise development in agribusiness and conservation. It has grown to become one of the leading enterprise development consulting firms in East Africa. The company is owned and operated by its consultant directors, who are responsible for overall policy decisions, management and operational guidelines. It has district contact agents who work part-time for the company and are paid per assignment. They maintain strategic links with 52 districts in Uganda.

ESDC serves a wide range of clients, including private-sector individuals, private companies, NGOs, community organizations, government ministries, local governments and other public-sector institutions, and various types of farmers' organizations.

Services

ESDC provides a range of services to its clients:

- **Market access.** This includes market research, promotion, information, and linkages such as exhibitions and exchange visits between producers and potential buyers.

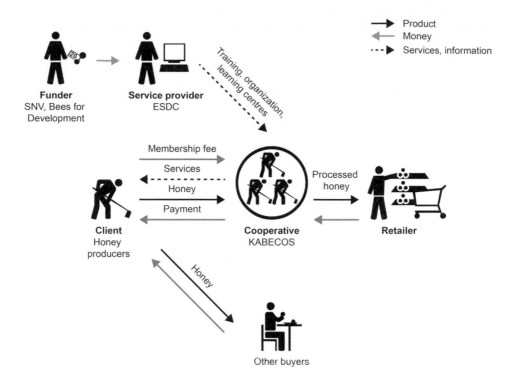

Figure 54　Simplified outline of how ESDC and KABECOS operate

- **Training and technical assistance.** This covers technical subjects as well as business management and entrepreneurship. It includes feasibility studies and business planning, management training, technical training, counselling and advisory services, legal services, financial and taxation advice, bookkeeping, strategic planning and strategy analysis.

- **Facilitating linkages between input suppliers and buyers.** This includes market linkages, access to information, facilitation of bulk buying, and improving a supplier's capacity to provide a regular supply of quality inputs.

- **Technology and product development.** This concerns the design, development and dissemination of appropriate technologies.

- **Product development and commercialization.** ESDC helps enterprises commercialize new products and services by assisting with product development, branding, market testing and initial marketing.

- **Business start-up support.** ESDC offers assistance to small and medium-sized businesses. It is the only group in Uganda to offer a wide range of professional support services to agricultural and forest-based small and medium-sized businesses and farmers.

- **Value-chain and sub-sector studies.** ESDC conducts analyses of value chains and industry sub-sectors. This has become common in recent years and is advocated by many as an excellent start for a development intervention or commercial investment.

- **Producer-group formation and strengthening.** ESDC supports commercially oriented producer organizations that provide services, generate economies of scale, and enable smallholders to overcome production and marketing constraints while managing natural resources.

Business models

ESDC has several types of business models.

Business model C1: Services paid by the client

In this model, companies hire ESDC to prepare business or strategic plans or marketing strategies for them. In addition, many individual landowners are employed outside agriculture and do not have the time or technical knowhow to set up their own farming business. ESDC does this for them: it agrees on a business, then plants, grows and sells on behalf of these individuals. This kind of work accounts for around half of ESDC's business-service turnover.

Figure 55   ESDC's business model C1

Business model A1: Government or donor pays for services to farmers

ESDC gets funds from different donors to provide back-up services to cooperatives and local NGOs supporting farmers. ESDC's services include entrepreneurship development, collective marketing, marketing linkages, and advice on technical production, cooperative management. Sometimes ESDC works with cooperative managers, sometimes directly with farmers. This business model accounts for around one third of the company's business-service turnover. However, it is the most profitable business model because it requires few inputs other than staff time. It was ESDC's first kind of business; the company later added the other models discussed below. ESDC's work with KABECOS is an example of this model.

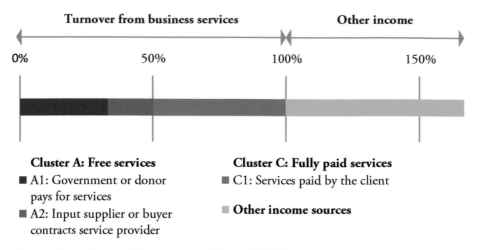

Turnover from business services   **Other income**

0%   50%   100%   150%

Cluster A: Free services
- A1: Government or donor pays for services
- A2: Input supplier or buyer contracts service provider

Cluster C: Fully paid services
- C1: Services paid by the client

- Other income sources

Figure 56   **Share of business models in ESDC's revenue**

Business model A2: Input supplier or buyer contracts service provider

ESDC works with individuals and companies (especially processors) that need raw materials to run their businesses. They hire ESDC to organize farmers to ensure a regular supply of materials. This is still a small part of the ESDC's work, accounting for around 15% of its business-service turnover.

Other sources of income

ESDC buys honey from farmers, turns it into honey wine, and sells it to high-end supermarkets. ESDC pays farmers more than the market price as a way to help those farmers to get additional income. This accounts for 40% of ESDC's total turnover.

Accountability

ESDC always conducts evaluations of its training. Participants are encouraged to speak out on things that may not be going well, and ESDC endeavours to respond to their concerns.

ESDC sees a consultancy as the initial phase of its relationship with its clients. It keeps them informed on progress and organizes meetings to review progress and decide on any changes needed. The company is committed to establish long-term links with its clients and to continue supporting them. It keeps a list of all its past and present clients and contacts them on a regular basis to check on their progress and to find out if they need additional services.

The company also keeps records of all the farmers it has worked with, follows up with them, and makes sure they know how to contact ESDC.

Sustainability

ESDC strives for sustainability by keeping a close eye on budgets and ensuring that its ventures are profitable. Its strategy is to keep operational costs very low, for instance by retaining a small core staff and engaging freelancers on an assignment-by-assignment basis.

ESDC invests in broadening its client base by following-up past and existing clients, responding to enquiries from visitors, and asking clients to recommend ESDC to others.

The company maintains several lines of business. For example, it buys honey from farmers, turns it into honey wine, and sells it to supermarkets.

Inclusiveness

The donors ESDC works for have different target groups they want to reach. This determines the people ESDC works with. Most of the company's work involves small-scale producers and small enterprises.

Lessons

Most of ESDC's assignments are generated through recommendations by past and current clients. Therefore, it is important to know the clients very well, keep them happy, stay in contact with them, offer additional services, etc. A key business strategy for business service providers is to get clients to recommend its work to others; that makes the business sustainable.

It is always better to engage clients directly in an assignment than to inform them through reporting. This not only saves time, but also creates direct interactions with the client, making it easier to reach agreements quickly on what direction to take. The client can provide direct feedback and has a clear idea about the expected results.

More information

www.esdconsults.com

http://apf-uganda.ning.com/group/effective-skills-development-consultants

Ambrose Bugaari, ambrose_bugaari@yahoo.com

The business of agricultural business services

From urban business consulting to rural business services: Target, Ethiopia

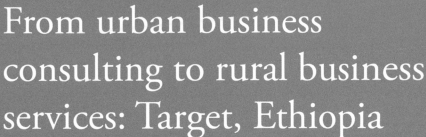

Transporting apples to market in Ethiopia
Photo: Target Business Consultants, Ethiopia

From urban business consulting to rural business services: Target Business Consultants, Ethiopia

Getnet Haile

Livestock are important in Hamer *woreda* in southern Ethiopia. They are a promising source of income for the future, too: domestic and international demand is high, and local pastoralists market their animals through various channels. But they benefit little because the value chains are inefficient, making the pastoralists reluctant to sell.

Pact Ethiopia, an American NGO, commissioned Target Business Consultants to conduct a study on livestock marketing in Hamer. Target used a participatory approach to study the value chain, then validated the findings and recommendations through a workshop involving pastoralists, service providers and government representatives. The resulting document was sent to policymakers and development organizations operating in the region. It recommended various interventions:

- Establishing alternative investment options for pastoralists, such as grain mills, water pumps for rent, and housing in small towns for rent.

- Establishing microfinance services as a way for pastoralists to save the income they earn from selling animals.

- Establishing cooperatives and enhancing their capacity, and building the capacity of offices to promote cooperatives.

- Establishing markets in selected villages.

- Establishing village cereal banks where pastoralists can trade livestock for grain.

Target Business Consultants

Studies like the one in Hamer are a growing line of business for Target, along with various other business services for rural clients. Target was founded in 2004 by two business and financial specialists, Getnet Haile and his wife, Woderyelesh Habtihun. They saw the rising demand for financial management services among NGOs and the private sector. They invested their savings in the new firm.

The company has grown steadily over time and now provides a range of business services: training, coaching and mentoring on financial management, business planning, taxation, accounting software, value chain studies, organizational system development, including human resources, financial management, procurement, and marketing. Its clients include NGOs, businesses, government, international organizations and cooperatives. Currently, Target has eight permanent staff and about 20 freelancers. Professionally, the staff and the freelancers have backgrounds in business management, marketing, agricultural economics, accounting, information technology and animal sciences.

Target started out providing services such as accounting, computerization of accounting systems, developing financial management manuals, and training. Later it added business planning and marketing services. It used to focus solely on urban areas, until 2007 when it did its first rural-oriented assignment for an apple-growing cooperative (see Box 9). This was a new area for Target, so it took longer than expected. But the results were fascinating for both the Target team and the cooperative.

As a result, Target stepped up its work in rural development. It coached 18 farmers' organizations on financial management and business planning in a multiannual value chain development programme (Belt and Goris 2011). Target took a deeper interest in value chain development and secured work in livestock and gums and resin value chains and later on in the dairy, oilseeds, honey, grains and vegetables chains.

Target now has a customized training package for cooperatives, dealing with entrepreneurship, marketing, financial management and organizational management. It has also developed a financial management manual for medium-sized cooperatives which can easily be adapted to specific needs of individual cooperatives.

Box 9   Apples in Chencha

Chencha woreda (district) is one of Ethiopia's few apple-growing areas. But the local apple-growers' cooperative, the Chencha Highland Fruits Marketing Cooperative, has experienced problems in expanding their production and marketing, even though Ethiopian apples are a lot cheaper than the imported fruit that dominate the market.

At the request of SNV, a Dutch development organization, Target has been assisting the cooperative to improve its operations. It helped develop a business plan, which included an advertising campaign to attract customers. This was successful: the cooperative's turnover increased tenfold between 2007 and 2008, and membership nearly doubled to 600. Eight other cooperatives of apple growers were formed in the Gamo Gofa Zone, of which Chencha is part.

But that led to new problems: the Chencha cooperative had grown too big to be run by volunteers, and members' commitment declined. Many sold their output to other buyers rather than channelling it through the cooperative.

After conducting a business diagnosis, Target recommended the cooperative hire a professional accountant and storekeeper. Performance improved as a result, with turnover rising from ETB 6 million in 2010–11 ($360,000) to ETB 8 million in 2011–12 ($440,000).

Business models

Business model C1: Services paid by the client

In this model, clients such as the government, a company or NGO pay Target for its services. This is Target's most important model in terms of overall income: 75% of its turnover falls in this category. Target envisages that this model will remain its most important source of income. The work in Hamer *woreda* described at the beginning of this case is an example, though most of Target's work in this model is outside agriculture.

Figure 57   Target's business model C1

Business model A1: Government or donor pays for services to farmers

Typically, a funder such as SNV (as in Chencha) contracts Target to provide services to cooperatives. Target is sometimes the only organization working with the cooperative; at other times it works in partnership with other consultancy companies. This is Target's second most important model in terms of turnover, accounting for about 15% of its

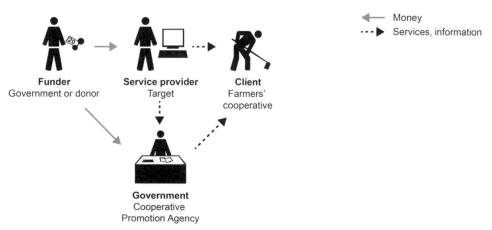

Figure 58   Target's business model A1

Box 10   Dida Cooperative Union

Dida Farmers' Cooperative Union was formed by a number of cooperatives of smallholder farmers. As it grew, the union could no longer handle its accounting and inventory management using a manual recording system. Symptoms of a weak financial management systems included backlogs in recording, the poor quality of reports, weak inventory and fixed asset control, and delays in reporting.

The union managed to secure funding from Agriterra to improve its financial management. It commissioned Target to study and improve its operations. Target developed a chart of accounts, along with a coding system for the inventory, customers, vendors and fixed assets. It trained Dida staff on the selected accounting system. After the training, it mentored the accountants for a period of 3 months – until they had worked off a year's backlog and produced proper financial and management reports from the system. The accountants managed to complete the following year's accounts in just 4 months.

revenue in 2011. All of this business is in the agricultural sector. When working under this business model, Target often plays the role of back-up service provider by supporting others in delivering services to farmers.

Business model A3: Vouchers for services

In this business model, a funder provides a client with resources, which then hires Target to perform a particular service. Target has so far done only two assignments in this category, both in agriculture. These were when Agriterra, a Dutch NGO, funded two cooperatives to develop their business plans (Box 10). This model accounts for about 5% of Target's turnover.

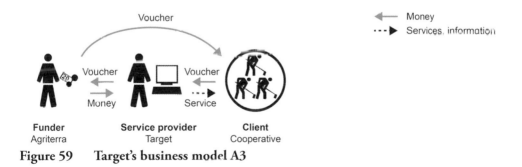

Figure 59   Target's business model A3

Business model B1: Part-payment by clients

Under this model, a donor (such as the International Trade Centre and the Centre for Development and Enterprise) hires Target to provide services to Ethiopian private

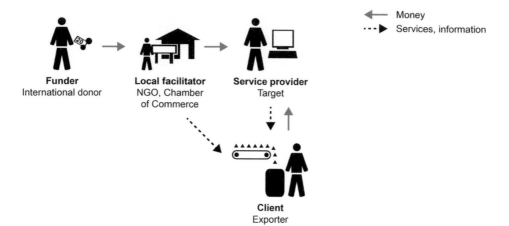

Figure 60   Target's business model B1

exporters. These clients may be large or small scale; they pay a fee that covers around 10–15% of Target's costs for the job. The rest is covered by the donor. This model accounts for about 5% of the company's turnover. None of the assignments have so far been in the agricultural sector.

Accountability

Target is accountable to both its funders (international donors, NGOs, etc.) and to its clients through evaluations and reports. Target sees client feedback as an important way to improve the quality of its services. It does evaluations each day during training and coaching activities.

Target monitors the results of its training and coaching after the assignment is over. It sees this as part of its "after-sales services". It calls clients to ask whether they are facing new challenges and how it can still help – at no extra cost. This has greatly helped Target to strengthen its networking and relationships with clients. Much of its repeat business has come from such after-sales services.

Sustainability

Target has a variety of donors and clients, making it financially more sustainable. Its training activities generate enough revenue to cover its costs, but it does not generate a profit. Training is nevertheless an important source of contacts for Target: people come for training, get interested in what the company does, and go back with ideas on how it could help them. Target therefore sees training as an important part of its business.

Target builds its clients' capacity to do things like business planning themselves. Once they have these skills, they no longer need Target's services in this area – though they may recall that Target did a good job and come back for assistance on something else.

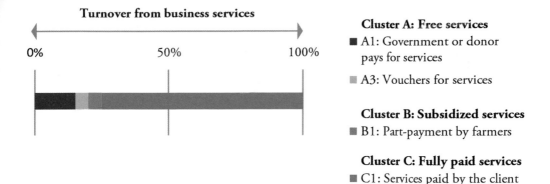

Turnover from business services

0%   50%   100%

Cluster A: Free services
- A1: Government or donor pays for services
- A3: Vouchers for services

Cluster B: Subsidized services
- B1: Part-payment by farmers

Cluster C: Fully paid services
- C1: Services paid by the client

Figure 61   Share of business models in Target's revenue

Target organizes in-house training for its own staff to promote internal exchange and learning and to keep up with new client demands. The objective is to increase the quality of the company's services and to develop new products. These new products are a direct response to the challenges that Target staff see when working with clients. A good example is a new course on "practical financial analysis", which grew out of the realization that managers spend a lot of time and energy on producing traditional financial data (such as gross profits), rather than understanding what these figures say. The course trains managers and accountants to "read behind the data", analysing trends and unravelling reasons why results change. Target has already taught this course in four companies and expects more to follow soon.

Inclusiveness

How inclusive is Target in its work? That depends on the funder. All the cooperatives that Target works with are made up of smallholders. Cooperatives have a lot of demands in organizational development: financial management, a stock-management system, or training in certain technical topics. But small cooperatives cannot afford to pay Target, so they have to rely on financial support from donors.

Target customizes its trainings to suit the skills and capacities of the participants and to make sure they will help them solve their problems. For example, it can also train illiterate individuals on financial management and entrepreneurship.

Challenges and opportunities

The current business environment in Ethiopia is good: the private sector is growing. NGOs are getting more involved in private-sector development too. Plus, international donors are interested in working with the private sector to promote market-oriented agriculture. There is an important shift from donor grants for food security and technical assistance towards developing market linkages. New private-sector actors need first to comply with laws on civil society and taxation, and then be ready to confront the competition. All of this means there are plenty of opportunities for Target.

But there are challenges too. One is the high turnover of cooperative and private-sector staff. Target often trains people who then leave their organization, and it needs to start from scratch again.

Another challenge relates to the use of freelancers. Target hires them to fill gaps in capacity or knowledge that are not part of Target's core business, or simply to cope with a lot of assignments at the same time. These freelancers do not take part in the standard cycle of learning and sharing within Target. Target finds it hard to ensure that freelancers deliver the quality that Target insists on. Target keeps a close watch on these freelancers and hires them again only if they have fulfilled their tasks properly.

Target plans to redesign its training and coaching methodologies so they can be provided at lower cost without compromising quality. It hopes to outsource some services to regional consultants to improve outreach and cut transport costs. The lower the cost of delivering the service, the greater is the likelihood that it will be adopted on a wide scale.

Lessons

Target has shifted its focus from urban to rural. It finds agriculture more satisfying and stimulating. Its agriculture-related business has grown from zero in 2005 to 25% of its revenue in 2012.

Through its extensive work in rural communities, Target has been able to demystify seemingly complicated subjects such as financial management, marketing and organizational management. It has developed courses that can be understood easily by farmers. Customized quality services and after-sales service have improved Target's links with its clients and funders and led to repeated business. Some clients specifically ask their donors to choose for Target when they want to support them.

More information

www.targetethiopia.com

Getnet Haile, getnet@targetethiopia.com

7 Analysis

It is important to ensure that business services benefit women and disadvantaged people
Photo: Harun Thomas, FFARM, Ethiopia

7   Analysis

The 12 cases in Chapter 4–6 tell the stories of business service providers that are more or less successful. This chapter draws on them, and on discussions among their authors, to derive lessons about the providers. The analysis is organized in four areas: financial sustainability, accountability, inclusiveness and capacity development (see also Chapter 3).

Financial sustainability

The service providers face a number of issues in maintaining their financial sustainability:

Who pays? Larger farmers and other actors in the value chain are likely to be willing and able to pay for services. Some smallholder farmers will pay too if they find the services to be of value to them. Many others, in contrast, are unable to pay in full for a large number of services.

Overdependence on a single source of income. A service provider that relies too much on one donor, a particular crop or type of client, or a single line of business may lose out if the donor's whim changes or a particular type of service becomes less relevant.

Short-term, small-scale projects. Many projects are short-term in nature. But service providers need to earn an income after they finish. In addition, the scale of certain services is limited because the markets for them are small. There is often little room for efficiency driven by economies of scale. Effective services need to be tailor-made to meet the specific demands of clients. That makes providing business services more costly than, for example, microfinance, which largely follow a standard methodology.

Uneven playing field. In principle, competition between service providers is generally considered to be positive. It raises the quality of service provision, and reduces service prices. But it can have adverse effects, such as harming collaboration between the providers, reducing the exchange of knowledge and investment in new services.

Although some service providers complain about increasing competition, they also say there are plenty of opportunities. Their concerns are rather with the uneven playing field: they say that different tax rules for private companies and NGOs result in unfair competition. Some governments control key functions in the chain of staple foods and cash crops they regard as "strategic". The government in Uganda, for example, controls smallholder cotton; in Zambia, maize; in Ghana, cocoa; and in Rwanda, potatoes. Private service providers have a hard time entering such commodity chains.

Development vs commercial interests. A number of private service providers also have development goals: they might be characterized as "social enterprises". These development goals require a different mindset from the same enterprises' commercial goals, and the two types of goals may have conflicting implications for the way the service providers are organized and operate. For-profit service providers are organized to provide efficient services to paying clients. These services are often of a different character from those offered to smallholders who have (at least initially) difficulty in paying. They may call for staff with different competencies and talents. These two worlds, development and commercial, are not necessarily mutually exclusive, though, as for-profit business activities can subsidize development-oriented activities.

We look at the issue of financial sustainability from two angles:

- General strategies put in place by service providers to remain in business

- Strategies for continued service provision to smallholders in particular.

General strategies

Service providers respond to the challenges outlined above in a number of ways. Below are issues of importance to all providers, regardless of their business model and target clientele.

Quality control. Service providers need to maintain a reputation for quality. The funder's willingness to hire them depends on their ability to deliver quality services. Target and Bindzu, for example, take client satisfaction very seriously: they ask their clients for feedback after each milestone in service delivery (see below on *Accountability*). Target has a professional system of internal learning and quality assurance, supported by clear internal procedures.

Staffing. Several service providers maintain a small number of core staff, and hire freelancers when necessary to fill in gaps in staffing or expertise. This makes it possible to expand at short notice to take advantage of new opportunities, and to pay the freelancers only when they are needed. But it can be hard to find suitably qualified freelancers, and there may be problems in quality control (local consultants in the case of Target, local extension agents in the case of Excel Hort).

Short- and long-term contracts. A number of cases mention the need to balance long- and short-term contracts to ensure that the company has a steady financial base from which to operate and innovate. This is the case for Miruku, which has its fixed costs covered for the next three years through a long-term project. This was only possible through good financial management: Miruku recently revised its financial management system so as to be able to trace costs and income from its business versus not-for-profit activities.

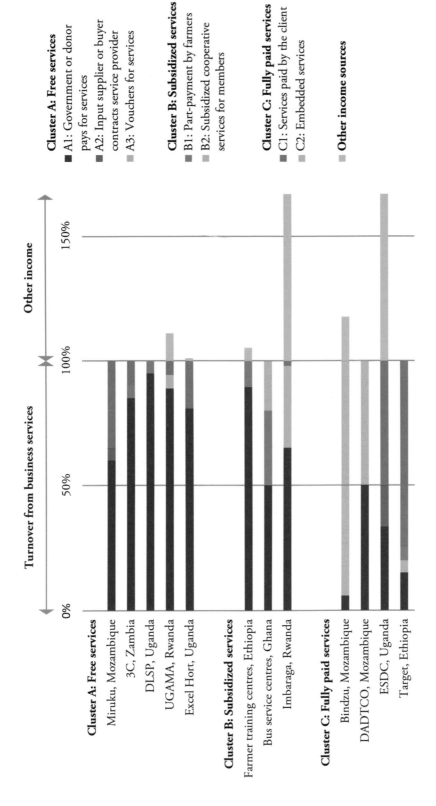

The business of agricultural business services

Figure 62   Proportion of different business models for different providers, based on estimated business service revenue in 2012

Figure 63 Private service providers maintain their financial sustainability by following multiple business models and having several sources of income

A combination of models. All the service providers in this book operate a mix of business models (Figure 62). The most common by far is the donor-pays model (model A1): it accounts for an average of 60% of the business-service revenues of the 12 providers, and for 50% or more of the revenue of nine of the 12 cases. It accounts for 95% of DLSP's enterprise grant programme in Uganda (though this is only part of DLSP's work). At the other end of the scale, this model accounts for only 6% of the revenues of Bindzu in Mozambique.

None of the other business models accounts for more than 20% of the total. Certain business models are important for individual service providers, though. For example, embedded services (model C2) account for over 80% of Bindzu's revenues, and 50% of DADTCO's.

All of the service providers operate between two and four different business models. They do this for various reasons: to spread their risk, to earn income or recoup costs, in response to donor policies, to take advantage of opportunities that have arisen, etc.

Different funders. Spreading risk by having contracts with different donors is a common strategy among the service providers (Excel Hort, DADTCO, Bindzu, Target, Imbaraga, ESDC). They maintain a portfolio of different funders: not only international NGOs and the government, but also private-sector input suppliers, entrepreneurs, and small and large farmers.

Relations with donors. A number of service providers work constantly on maintaining and improving their relations with donors; after all, these are by far their most important sources of revenue. Miruku and Target mention that networking, meetings and presentations are very important to maintain and expand their client base. They help in getting their companies' names known, attracting new donors and reminding previous donors that they are still in business. The strategy seems to pay off, as both companies have a number of returning clients.

A general risk is that donor's priorities change frequently, sometimes forcing projects to end abruptly (see, for example, the case of Bindzu, which almost went bankrupt because of the sudden withdrawal of a donor). But private-sector partners can also be risky: Bindzu's main supplier, Omnia, has stopped providing it with inputs on credit, and has set up a competing outlet nearby.

Generalization, not specialization. Some service providers say they have unique selling points – such as quality and innovativeness. But it is unclear how far these really distinguish these providers from the competition. Although some hint at some kind of specialization (e.g., ESDC), all service providers in this book provide a range of services and serve different clients. There is little sign of profound specialization. On the contrary: hiring freelancers, for example, is often used as means to reach for new fields. Staying as a generalist makes a business more financially sustainable, judging by the cases in this book.

Keeping innovative. Constant revision and, if needed, upgrading of a business model, is crucial if a service provider is to become and remain competitive. To do this, service providers need to understand agricultural trends and what their clients require. They need to strategically plan, innovate and differentiate their services. They need to build strategic alliances.

By analysing their business models, service providers can see where their activities need upgrading. Doing so ensures that they can meet their customer expectations, improve their efficiency, and become a reliable and profitable supplier of services. Many of the private-sector providers in this book already do a simplified form of such an analysis.

Entering the value chain. Service providers often engage directly in the value chain: they buy or sell produce, process raw materials, etc. Five of the 12 service providers do this, seeing it as an important way to ensure financial sustainability and manage risks. When buying or selling, some (e.g., Bindzu and DADTCO) also provide information and advice as added value. This is what we call "embedded" services (see Chapter 6).

Other companies simply buy, process and sell a product, and reinvest the profit generated in the company. This is the case for ESDC (which buys honey and turns it into wine), Excel Hort (which makes tree-tomato wine) and Bindzu (which grows sugarcane and horticultural products). The farmer training centres in Ethiopia recover part of their costs by selling produce and seed produced by community labour. DADTCO buys cassava and processes it: this is the company's main line of business; it sees itself as a processor rather than a service provider. UGAMA has recently taken shares in a rice mill and an input company, aiming to reinvest any profits in UGAMA itself. Two companies offer non-agricultural services to bolster their financial sustainability: both Imbaraga and Target rent out their training facilities.

Besides generating income, such activities bring the organization in contact with new potential partners and clients, so creating opportunities for new assignments. Being directly involved in the value chain gives the company first-hand experience of markets, postharvest handling and processing. They are therefore well placed to help farmers and other local actors to improve their practices.

Strategies for continued service provision to smallholders

Some services do not have to be provided on a sustainable basis. Target, for example, trains cooperatives to develop their own business plans. Once they know how to do this, they no longer need the same service; they may instead need a different type of service altogether, or no service at all. The objective of such one-off services is to make farming more profitable and sustainable, not to sustain the service itself. If some follow-up is needed, this can be less intensive than the initial input, and the clients may be able to pay for at least part of the cost. Imbaraga, for example, relies on membership fees to maintain the services it offers its members.

Other types of service, such as market information or enterprise management, are needed on a longer-term or permanent basis. It is here that sustainability of provision becomes an issue.

Reaching larger farmers – who are often capable of paying for services – in a financially sustainable manner already requires a solid business strategy. Working with smallholders is much more challenging. Smallholders find it difficult to pay for services whose results they only see months later. Poorer farmers are often so cash-strapped that they are completely unable to pay.

In this section, we list a number of existing and potential strategies to ensure service providers can have smallholders as clients, and remain financially strong. We put these into four groups:

- Making free services available

- Partial payment by clients

- Full payment by clients

- Reducing the cost of services.

Making free services available to smallholders

For some services and certain areas, it is unrealistic to charge smallholders, so services have to be provided for free. This is the case of advice on production, for example; and for farmers in areas with little access to markets.

Possible ways of organizing this include:

- **Rely on public extension services.** Though subject to the whims of politics, public extension services are likely to be longer-term that international donor support for particular projects. An example is the activities of DLSP in Uganda.

- **Rely on NGOs.** They may be paid by government of donors to deliver services for free for farmers. Because the NGOs continue to depend on the funder, the sustainability of this strategy for service provision remains questionable.

Partial payment by clients

In other cases, it is expected that farmers will pay for at least part of the services they receive. Donors typically play an important role in early steps of service delivery, and gradually reduce their contribution.

This can be done in several ways (various combinations are possible):

- **Gradual cost recovery.** Farmers start out by getting the service for free (or by paying a small amount), but each year they are charged a little more until they cover the full cost. One approach is to offer, for a small fee, introductory services that produce a quick payoff. Another is to give out vouchers that farmers can use to pay for part of the cost of a service. The value of the voucher declines gradually over time, so the farmer has to pay a larger share of the cost.

- **In-kind and material contributions.** Often, farmers are required to provide labour or building materials in return for a service. In the farmer training centres in Ethiopia, for example, farmers invest their time and resources to produce seed and other products. That stimulates their feeling of ownership for the centre. The products are sold to generate income to cover the training centres' expenses.

- **Rely on farmers' organizations to provide services.** Farmers' organizations usually charge their members a membership fee. They use this money to provide members with training and other services. The fees are rarely enough to cover the full costs of the services, so the organization has to seek donor support for the rest. This is the case, for example, of Imbaraga.

Full payment by clients

Private service providers may sell services at full cost or profitable prices. They may charge the full amount straight away, or they may do so after a transition period of partial payment. Possible strategies to reach full payment include:

- **Start with services that have a quick payback.** This can work for certain services (e.g., supporting negotiations with buyers), but not for others (e.g., advice on production).

- **Offer services in small packages.** Instead of running a 2-week workshop, a provider may offer several shorter seminars.

- **Payment by results.** Here, the farmers get the services and pay only when they see the results. For example, they may pay for production advice if their yields actually go up at the end of the season; they may pay for market advice if they manage to get a better price. This is not easy to put into practice as it needs some kind of benchmark or control to measure the improvement against. For such a model to work, a specific type of business or value chain is needed. It is unlikely to be possible with spot markets, where farmers do not have a prearranged buyer. But it may be possible if the buyer is contracted. That is often the case with commodities such as cotton or export crops.

- **Offer services on credit.** This is a related strategy, but is not without risks. Bindzu's attempt to supply inputs and services to small farmers on credit proved such a disaster that it decided to accept up-front payments only.

- **Support clients to find the resources to pay for the services.** This can be done by offering gradual payment mechanisms such as instalment payments or offering financing to allow the more vulnerable farmers to pay for services. The business service centres in Ghana have done this successfully by attaching the purchase of inputs to access to credit.

- **Embedded services.** Embedded services, where farmers get a service (such as advice) if they buy a product (such as fertilizer), have the potential to reach smallholders because they are not fee-based. To reach the more vulnerable smallholders, the services must be embedded in transactions that the farmers are likely to do (like selling cassava – and not buying a tractor).

- **Third-party payment.** Another financial sustainability strategy is to identify and deliver business services that are mutually beneficial to both small and large farms or firms, and charge only the large firms. This is what we referred to in this book as business model A2, which is followed by Miruku and ESDC (see Figure 8).

- **Piggybacking on microfinance.** Successful microfinance programmes often use credit meetings to disseminate information about a business service, but offer it as a separate, non-required, fee-based activity. The loan officers and service providers' staff are usually separate as well. The main advantages of this strategy is that clients have already access to finance to pay for services, and the costs of marketing services are smaller because clients are already coming together for loan committee meetings, for example. The disadvantages include the fact that farmers may feel pushed to take the services thinking their application for a loan will not be accepted otherwise, and the (often unrealistic) need to have staff knowledgeable on both microfinance and business development.

Reducing the cost of services

Lowering the cost of services makes it possible to reach more smallholders because it leads to more efficient service provision. In the longer run, lower costs and higher demand encourage more providers to enter the business. Reducing costs supports any of the strategies described above for free, partially paid or fully paid services. The more efficient the service provider, the cheaper and more affordable to farmers the services become.

Possible strategies include:

Specializing on particular tasks. In this case, NGOs, local governments or donors perform much of the business service development and testing – an expensive part of the business – with public resources. The private service providers merely adapt and implement, providing standard services that are cheaper for the end-client.

Direct costs can be further reduced if back-up service providers liaise between service providers and donors. Some service providers become experts at serving farmers, while a back-up provider (another NGO or a private company) specializes in negotiating and managing donor funds and developing supplier capacity. The donor or a back-up provider may also cover the costs of market research and provide technical assistance. These examples belong to the market-driven model of intervention described in Chapter 2.

Support with promotion. The funder may support a business service provider by promoting its services to clients or in new areas. That brings the service provider more clients, and reduces its costs of seeking new business.

Farmers as advisors. In some of the cases in this book, the goal is to build the capacity of the farmers so they can take over providing the services. In these cases, the service provider trains only a small number of farmer advisors; they go on to train their friends and neighbours. Excel Hort's potato growers are a good example of this. The hope is that Excel Hort will be able to establish a system that the farmers can manage in the future. Another example is DADTCO, which relies on the services of "lead farmers" to coordinate a network of cassava suppliers. A third example is ESDC's work with the KABECOS beekeeping cooperative. All three rely on a combination of donor-paid initial training, and voluntarism and self-interest among the farmers. It is hoped that the farmers will see it as in their own interests to get organized to keep producing potatoes, cassava or honey of the quality that the buyer demands.

A related strategy is to rely on trained farmers to become private service providers in their own right, paid either partly or totally by clients.

Working with groups. Working with a group is cheaper and easier than working with the same number of people individually. It is advantageous for the farmers to buy the service

> **Box 11   Key lessons and arguments from the cases: Sustainability**
>
> General strategies by service providers to sustain their business:
> - Ensure a variety of funders (NGOs, public, private).
> - Ensure a broad base of clients (small and medium enterprises, NGOs, small and large farmers).
> - Focus on quality as a way to retain old clients and get new ones.
> - Use networking to meet new clients and regain the interest of old ones.
> - Employ staff in a flexible way to respond to opportunities.
> - Keep overhead and investment costs low. Where possible, overhead costs related to donor liaison, marketing and research can be absorbed by other service providers (NGOs, donors).
> - Find ways to share the burden of payment with farmers (build local ownership): fees in cash and kind, taking over some of the services, economies of scale.
> - Separate the business and NGO-type activities, the former can fund the second where needed and desired.

as a group and get a discount for doing so. This point will be discussed further under *Inclusiveness* below.

Cross-subsidy. A service provider may offer some services at a loss, and subsidize them with income it earns elsewhere. It may do so for various reasons: a desire to serve small-scale farmers, because it is required to do so by the donor, or because it sees the smallholders as valuable future clients.

There are a number of ways how this can be organized. A service provider may operate an unrelated business and use its profits to subsidize a loss-making service. It may charge large farmers for a service, and use the profits to provide the same service at a lower price to small scale farmers. Or it may be able to provide the service at a lower price because the donor is covering the overhead or other costs.

Such cross-subsidies are a disadvantage for other service providers because they make it harder for them to compete. Such distortions of the market for business services can be avoided or minimized by donors and governments providing support to back-up service providers. These then support the service providers that deliver the services to the clients.

The main strategies used by the cases in this book to ensure sustainability of their businesses are highlighted in Box 11.

Changing mindsets

As can be seen from the many strategies described in this section, the move towards payment requires coordination among different actors in the extension system, from local governments to international donors and farmer organizations. This will be further explored in Chapter 8.

For a move towards partial or full payment by clients to work, a change in mindset is needed among service providers, clients and donors.

The service providers are used to getting paid to give away services for free. Most providers depend on donors (aid agencies, international NGOs or the government), which pay them to render services to farmers. Most of our cases depend largely on this business model (see Figure 62).

Farmers and other value chain actors are used to getting services for free. They need to know why a change is needed. A good strategy is to ensure that clients "own" the initiative or programme that provides the services. If they help manage the initiative (which takes time and capacity building), they will more easily accept a gradual increase in payments.

Donors are also used to the idea of providing services for free. Organizing payments is an administrative hassle and takes time that many projects do not have. And if other programmes in the same area provide services for free, clients are unlikely to accept the need to pay.

Accountability

By "accountability", we mean the way that the clients and other outsiders can have a say on the services that the clients receive. Mechanisms may range from informal feedback to formal monitoring and evaluation, withdrawal of funding or patronage, management control, or legal sanction. What happens as a result is also important: does this feedback have any effect on the service and how it is delivered?

We here discuss two types of accountability: upward and downward. We pay more attention to the latter.

Upward accountability

This is the service provider's accountability to the funder. In practice, service providers tend to be primarily accountable to those who pay their bills. In the most common models (business models A and B: free and subsidized services), the main funders (the government or donors) are different from the clients. This leads the providers to generate reports and other information that the funder requests, but to pay much less attention to feedback from farmers. This contradiction was clearly seen in the cases in this book.

Voucher systems (business model A3) are sometimes seen as an alternative: the donor pays, but clients choose the providers, so have a direct say about the quality and variety of services they use. But using vouchers is not a flawless strategy: there is not always a range of providers to choose from, and the system may be poorly managed. In the Zambia Development Agency's scheme (see the case of 3C), the farmers were under pressure to choose a particular provider, or connived with them to share the money once the vouchers were cashed. Bindzu (in Mozambique) was less critical of the system: it has served a substantial number of farmers who received government vouchers for inputs.

Figure 64   **Downward accountability means that the clients (farmers) have some control over the business services**

Service providers are also accountable to the government. Most obviously, they must comply with the law. But they must also fulfil various administrative requirements: they may have to be registered, comply with quality requirements or standards, submit to inspections, possess certificates or licenses to operate, demonstrate that their staff are suitably qualified, etc. Unfortunately, such governmental requirements tend to involve a lot of red tape and focus little on quality.

As an alternative to governmental control, service providers may be accountable to an association of business service providers or another accreditation system, such as the one piloted by 3C.

Downward accountability

Downward accountability is the service provider's accountability to the client. In the business models in our Cluster C, the clients pay for the service, so have a degree of control over the service provided. If they don't like it, they can refuse to pay, or they can "vote with their feet": they can stop using the service, refuse to come to meetings, and try to get the same service somewhere else.

Ideally, accountability is closely related to monitoring and evaluation, and should be a learning process: by listening to what clients have to say about their service, the providers can change and get better at what they do. We discuss here various ways the organizations in this book have tried to ensure downward accountability.

Determining needs. Ideally, farmers should be in a position to choose which service provider and services they want. In practice, there are very few alternatives, and many funders and service providers pay too little attention to understanding what farmers need, what they appreciate, and what they do not. This is especially the case where services are provided for free.

There are exceptions: Imbaraga is a farmer cooperative governed by its members, who are also the clients of its services (though the internal governance of farmer organizations is often far from perfect, and the organizations are sometimes controlled by a few better-off, typically male farmers). 3C and Excel Hort both carry out needs assessments before they start to work with a specific group. 3C goes further, by facilitating participatory planning sessions. ESDC has inception meetings to discuss its terms of reference with the clients, in addition to mid-term and end-of-project assessment meetings. Miruku has meetings with farmers to assess the company's performance. Excel Hort has a checklist to be used in similar meetings. In the case of DLSP, the projects supported come from the farmers' own ideas.

Formal agreements. Signing a memorandum of understanding with clients is one way to ensure some level of accountability and transparency. Such agreements can specify performance expectations, monitoring requirements, and perhaps payment depending on performance. But they are not yet common: often a "contract" is made with a handshake, as sometimes happens with Imbaraga. DLSP signs contracts with farmers' organizations (farmers pay for part of the services provided). SNV (a Dutch development organization which hires Target) asks clients to sign that they have received services as a condition for payment.

A tripartite agreement between donors, service providers and clients can be developed, for example at the inception meeting of a project. But merely signing a contract is not enough. Close monitoring in the field remains important. So does enforcement. Particularly in countries where judicial systems are dysfunctional, trust relations tend to be more effective than formalized ones.

Monitoring by donor. At times the donors take the responsibility to check with the clients about their satisfaction. The World Cocoa Foundation, for example, periodically holds focus-group discussions with farmers to monitor the performance of the business centres in Ghana. FAO (a donor of Excel Hort) and IFAD (which supports DLSP) employ independent consultants who monitor these organizations' performance by interviewing farmers and other clients.

Such an independent check – as well as internal auditing and accounting – enhances accountability. But these tend to be expensive, affordable only by external donors.

Feedback from clients. Where clients pay directly for services, or where they contribute part of the cost, accountability tends to be much less problematic, as the client has a direct say on what service is provided, and what he or she thinks of it. The business service

Box 12   Key lessons and arguments: Accountability

Strategies to strengthen downward accountability:
- Strengthen client-orientation of service provision by giving clients a direct say in the services beforehand (through needs assessment), during and after services are provided.
- Ensure clients have a role in monitoring the quality of services, through frequent checks (meetings, discussions, community scorecards, etc.). These checks can be simple and do not need to make services more expensive.
- Especially where services are paid by donors, make sure these checks are done either directly by clients or by an independent third party.

centres in Ghana, for example, are accountable to the farmer groups through community facilitators. Their strategy is to disclose all information and criteria regarding each service, especially the fee-based services that farmers have to pay for.

From the point of view of accountability, it is therefore important that the clients have some control over the funding for the service. They may contribute their own resources (in cash or in kind), or the donor may give them control over some of its resources (as in voucher schemes, business model A3). Where the local government provides the services, clients may be able to exert influence via the political process, but in practice this is not always the case.

Figure 65   Inclusiveness means serving all types of farmers, including the poor, the disadvantaged, and women

From the 12 cases in this book, we can conclude that private-sector providers (especially those that offer services fully paid by clients) have a stronger record in monitoring the quality of their own services, and in feeding that information back into their own organizations. They have stronger incentive to be more demand-oriented. Box 12 brings together some lessons from the cases in this book on downward accountability.

Inclusiveness

In most of sub-Saharan Africa, smallholders produce the bulk of farm output but supply a much smaller share of the marketed produce (World Bank 2007). Helping smallholders become more market and business-oriented is a challenge for business service providers. It is not just a question of getting them to produce and sell more. The farmers also need to serve urban, regional and international markets – markets that are changing rapidly. They may have to intensify and mechanize their production, switch to new crops or livestock products, specialize, add value by processing, and produce and sell at a larger scale. That requires new skills in production, organization, management and marketing.

Business service providers work mostly with commercial farmers. There are many challenges in serving smallholder subsistence farmers, particularly those who derive little income from any surpluses they may grow. If they do not run their farms as businesses, they are not likely to request business services… and if they do not see the need for business services, they will certainly not pay for them. A large number of these farmers live in remote areas, with little infrastructure and no organized market.

Here are some ways service providers in this book try to reach smallholders, both subsistence and those who are more commercially oriented.

Working with groups

One way of serving smallholders is to work with groups and associations of farmers. Almost all the organizations described in this book did this; an exception was the farmer training centres in Ethiopia. In principle, groups can get access to inputs, credit and markets more easily than individuals because of economies of scale and the capacity to negotiate. That makes it possible for individual members to intensify their production. Farmers' groups can also specialize, use machinery and add value to their produce.

Inclusiveness is related to the composition of the groups. In general, highly commercial groups tend not to include subsistence farmers. A business-oriented group may exclude some categories of farmers, either directly (because they do not meet the criteria for membership), or indirectly (they cannot afford the membership fee or buy shares). Monitoring the composition of the groups seems important – but is rare in our cases.

Almost all the service providers in the cases work with groups of smallholders (for example, DLSP, Miruku, DADTCO and Excel Hort). Donor-funded programmes often make working with groups a condition for an intervention. Some of the service providers focus on groups that are already market-oriented before they receive support (DLSP), while others also work specifically with vulnerable groups (3C). In some cases, clusters of informal groups develop into a cooperative enterprise. Most of the groups that appear in the cases have individual membership. Some service providers (ESDC, for example) aim at household rather than individual membership. This distinction may have gender implications that are worth exploring. Considering households as members means that women are almost always also part of the group.

Imposing criteria for selecting clients

Donors may impose criteria for the types of farmers they want service providers to work with. They may impose selection criteria such as farm size, commodity type or market orientation. For example, they may want to support farmers in remote areas with few market opportunities, and those that grow food crops.

Some programmes tailor their approaches to make it easier for disadvantaged clients to use the services. For example, high levels of illiteracy have prompted the farmer training centres in Ethiopia to reach poorly educated farmers in special ways: demonstrations and study tours rather than training, or loudspeakers and community radio rather than billboards for market information.

To ensure that farmers without ready cash can benefit from fee-based services, the business service centres in Ghana and farmer training centres in Ethiopia accept payment in the form of labour. All other cases provide services for free to subsistence farmers, as well as to some newly commercial farmers.

Targeting women and young people

Many service providers try to target women and young people. In some countries that is difficult: few women attend trainings and meetings (e.g., in the business service centres in Ghana). It is easier in others: in the 3C case in Zambia, women are the majority. There are good reasons for this emphasis: women grow many staple food crops, as well as commercial vegetables and mushrooms; they also rear animals, process the harvest, and do much more. Plus, they often manage money better than men, and tend to be hard-working and committed (Box 13). Nevertheless, they are more often illiterate than male farmers. That

---

Box 13   Women can become entrepreneurs

"With training and support, women can become entrepreneurs and add value to the chain through creative ideas. In the process, their self-esteem and economic decision-making power increase. Training in production and business development can strengthen women's capacities to the point where they can take up leadership positions. When women have access to services and information, they can expand and improve their businesses"

Source: KIT, Agri-ProFocus and IIRR 2012

---

means that working with women requires different approaches. DLSP requires that women make up 30% of the members of each group it serves, and 30% of the group leaders must also be women. It uses a methodology called Gender Action Learning System, which emphasizes gender justice and ownership, and involves household monitoring.

Some of the service providers have special programmes for young farmers (Imbaraga) and people living with HIV or AIDS (3C).

Tailor services to the client

Subsistence farmers require different services from fully commercial farmers. Understanding its clientele is fundamental for any business. Establishing a relationship of trust with the clients and understanding their needs are essential to tailor services to different types of farmers.

Profitable clients vs inclusiveness

In promoting smallholder businesses, governments and donors often try to be as inclusive as possible, so that services reach the poor, women, and the disadvantaged. But the instincts of private-service providers lead them to serve clients who can pay for their services – which means better-off farmers who are able to take risks and operate in the same mindset as the service provider. The services demanded by this clientele are often very different than those required by subsistence farmers.

The organizations described in this book often do both: they work under contract with donors to provide services to smallholders who cannot pay for the services (or who can pay only part of the costs). They tailor these services carefully to the needs of these donors, sometimes requiring payment in kind by the clients. At the same time, they also work directly with larger farmers who are able to pay. This strategy has been discussed under *Sustainability* above.

The degree of inclusiveness depends on various issues:

- **The type of service.** Providing linkages to banks, for example, is more important for established and newly commercial farmers than for subsistence farmers. Providing support to farmers to get organized is often more important for subsistence and newly commercial farmers.

- **Gender sensitivity.** All types of services should be gender sensitive. It is necessary to take into consideration the division of tasks between men and women, the reasons for this division, and power issues within the household and the community.

- **The commodity.** This may have a big influence on the type of client. In many areas, cotton is grown by smallholders, while sugarcane is grown by commercial farmers. The choice of commodity thus has implications for the type of client and how inclusive the programme can be.

Box 14   Key lessons and arguments: Inclusiveness

Strategies for inclusiveness:
- Know your audience: understand very well the farmers that are targeted by a particular intervention or donor. Establish a relationship with them and let them influence the design of the services.
- Tailor services to the clients. Different clients need and want different services. A one-size-fits-all strategy is unlikely to work.
- Have a clear purpose in mind for an intervention: is it to comply with a donor request, to meet your own social responsibility ideals, or to cater to your business orientation? These elements weigh differently in the various cases: all are valid in their own right.
- Adapt payments to the client. Some clients can pay in cash; others can pay but will need credit to do so; others may be able to pay in kind, for example, by contributing labour or materials.
- Consider part-payments. For some types of service, it may not be feasible to charge the whole cost; consider instead charging a smaller sum and making up the shortfall in other ways – by embedding the service in the price of inputs, by cross-subsidizing activities, or by relying on donors to pay the difference.
- Provide space for both group and individual entrepreneurship.
- Empowering women and supporting them in developing their own businesses demands a good understanding of the different roles of men and women, the reasons for such differences, and the power dynamics within a group or a household.

- **Funding.** If resources are available from the government and donors to subsidize services, it is easier to target services to disadvantaged clients.

Box 14 summarizes some of the lessons on inclusiveness derived from the cases in this book.

Capacity development

There is clearly a demand for the types of services provided by the organizations (public, private and NGO) depicted in Chapters 4–6. Governments, donors and the private sector alike are interested in financing and delivering such services. But one of the major issues is the availability of qualified service providers.

The most relevant qualification for a manager of a service provider seems to be a master's degree in business administration or agricultural economics: five of the 12 managers who contributed to this book have such degrees (see the *Contributors' profiles* at the end of the book). The rest have qualifications in agriculture or related fields. Nevertheless, most have learned their jobs by doing them: they have had little or no specific training on business services. Despite this, they do feel that such training is important to develop their businesses further. How, then, to build the capacity of the service providers?

Doing so does not just mean introducing new tools and procedures to enhance their performance. Rather, service providers need to increase their capacity at various levels: institutional, organizational, and technical.

The institutional level refers to norms, policies and interaction patterns. Improving institutional capacity means, for example, enhancing the service providers' capacity to work and link with different organizations and cultures, or deepening their knowledge and understanding of local regulations. The organizational level refers to financial management and administration skills, human resources development, efficient and effective task distribution, selling services, and negotiating contracts. The technical level refers to the knowledge of technical issues at stake, be it land measurement or market analysis.

Institutional capacity

In terms of institutional capacity development, two major avenues emerge. The first related to the organization of service providers in some kind of association. We discuss this in Chapter 8.

The second refers to the establishment of links between service providers and universities and other training institutes. Some training institutes now offer mid-career professional courses – though these are not yet common. And universities are beginning to develop the courses needed to train business service providers, as mentioned in the UGAMA case.

The relationship between service providers and training institutes may well go beyond that of students and teachers. Service providers are well placed to bring real experiences to the training through practical guest lectures and by hosting interns. They may also take part in curriculum reviews.

Advocacy is still needed for national ministries of education and agriculture to include the required skills in the curricula of agricultural education and training institutions. This advocacy can be done by associations of service providers and educational institutes.

Organizational capacity

Service providers come into the field of service provision from different backgrounds. Some were established explicitly to offer business services in rural areas: this was true for five cases: 3C, Excel Hort, ESDC, Miruku, and the business service centres in Ghana. Others have moved into the field from other specializations: production (Bindzu and the farmer training centres in Ethiopia), processing (DADTCO), government (DLSP), organizing farmers (UGAMA and Imbaraga), and business services in urban areas (Target). Those organizations that were founded to provide business services have had to discover and develop the skills that they need. Those organizations that have moved in from other fields have had the additional task of reorienting their services and staff skills.

All in all, service providers face important challenges in internal organization and management, including financial management. This task is made more difficult by the different business models in place, and the fact that service providers need to deal with reporting, administrative and financial requirements from a wide range of donors and clients.

Technical capacity

The technical capacity required depends on the clients' needs. One option to understand clients' needs better is to look at market opportunities – to serve farmers and other value chains – and work backwards to define what skills are needed to tap into these opportunities. Some service providers use an internal SWOT analysis (Strengths, Weaknesses, Opportunities, Threats) to determine their priorities for capacity development (e.g., Miruku and Target).

Capacity needs also depend on the service provider's own field of expertise. Certain providers specialize in a certain product (such as cocoa, horticulture or honey), or in a certain transaction in the value chain (getting credit, buying, selling). Others focus on issues such as corporate social responsibility.

Service providers require skills and knowledge that are wide-ranging: from post-production, business planning and marketing, organization and finance, coordination and advocacy (see Box 2 in Chapter 1). In addition, the service provider must be adept at various assessment and delivery methods: facilitation, assessing needs, working with rural people from different ethnic and linguistic groups and educational backgrounds, approaching potential clients, writing proposals, communicating with donors and bankers organizing farmers' groups, selling services, training, coaching, mentoring, etc.

These skills should be part and parcel of formal training for service providers (public, non-profit or private). To do so, it would have to become part of the agriculture curriculum at technical and higher education institutes in developing countries.

Even if that does happen, it is unlikely that any one staff member, or indeed any one organization, can offer all the skills listed above. A few cases mention a division of labour between various service providers: one focuses on production training, another delivers business advice, a third arranges loans, and a fourth offers specialist mapping services (as in the business service centres in Ghana). More often, though, service providers continue to bet on generalization rather than specialization, making use of freelancers to cover areas they are not experts on.

Training for service providers

Training for service providers must be tailored to their current knowledge and skills. It should be practical and regular, and build on the experience of trainees, linking theory and practice to enable participants to put their new skills immediately into practice. Training should also be provided for field workers in doses that are manageable in combination with their routine work.

Box 15   Key lessons and arguments: Capacity development

Capacity development-aimed efforts requires:
- At the technical level, a mix of skills and qualifications that covers agronomic practices, economics, administration, process facilitation, community organization, value-chain development. This should be incorporated into technical agricultural curricula.
- Training tailor-made to both market opportunities and trainees' current capacities.
- Learning-by-doing, practice-oriented training methodology.
- Training materials based on real-life cases and that build on the trainees' experiences.
- Direct contact with local entrepreneurs and business service providers, who can be involved in the training and practical activities.
- Regular training, with good-quality follow up and on-the-job coaching during the gaps.
- Local back-up service providers to train and coach other service providers.
- Lobbying and advocacy from service providers to make it happen!

Training and learning can also be done internally: Target, for example, has an internal arrangement through which staff can learn for each other. The farmer training centres in Ethiopia arrange cross-visits for staff of one centre to learn from other centres that have been particularly successful.

Private service providers have limited opportunities to attend training sponsored by the public sector. And anyway, training programmes for the public sector still focus strongly on production rather than business, and need to be revised. Making public-sector resources available for private-sector service development has remained a sensitive issue in many countries. The private sector is often seen as making enough money already, and not as an appropriate recipient of public support. Some public-sector programmes (in Mozambique and Uganda, for example) provide investment matching funds (25% or 50%) for training local service providers (Heemskerk and Davis 2012).

NGOs have also been developing the capacity and skills of local private-sector service providers. But NGOs are often faced with capacity gaps of their own, and need staff training, particularly in enterprise development and marketing.

Various international agencies offer training in subjects such as financial management and cooperative business management. While valuable, such training tends to be one-off. Service providers also need help with implementing plans, follow-up, monitoring, and facilitating organizational or institutional change. These subjects call for more continuous and regular on-the-job coaching. This is better done by local back-up service providers: i.e., providers (often from the private sector) that offer training and support to other service providers. Target, Miruku and 3C offer such services.

8 Towards a needs-driven model

Learning how to use computers and the internet
Photo: IPMS, Ethiopia

8   Towards a needs-driven model

This chapter discusses what we envisage as a needs-driven model for service provision, and offers some recommendations to governments and donors on how to support such a model.

In Chapter 2 we explained the history of agricultural business development services. We described what Kahan (2007 and 2011) has labelled the **supply-driven** and **market-driven** models (Table 4).

In the **supply-driven model**, the funder (the government or a donor agency) decides what services to provide to farmers. The funder either delivers these services directly (for example, through the government extension system), or pays a private service provider or NGO to do so.

In the **market-driven model**, funders support the development of a market for business services. They can do so by supporting business development services to develop and commercialize their products, or by providing resources to potential clients to hire service providers, for example.

With our understanding of the 12 service providers depicted in this book, we can confidently say that these two models co-exist. The 12 cases tell more and less successful stories of business services that have improved the lives of the farmers they serve. But there is still plenty of room for improvement in the way these services are offered and delivered to farmers, farmers' associations and small and medium enterprises. The previous chapter discussed some ways to do this.

This chapter discusses how a support system for service providers must be put in place for the efforts of donors, governments and private sector providers to be fruitful. We argue that a third generation of business development services – a third model – is needed to answer to challenges faced by service providers and at the same time respond to the needs of smallholders and local value chain actors. We call this a **needs-driven model**. This does not mean merely that the supply-driven and market-driven models co-exist. It implies a different way to organize, support and deliver business services, paying particular importance to accountability, inclusiveness and sustainability.

Such a model would balance services for those who can pay all or part of the cost, with services for those who cannot. It would use donor and government resources wisely to ensure appropriate services to those who cannot pay, without crowding out the market for

Table 4   Characteristics of the supply-, market- and needs-driven models

	Supply-driven	Market-driven	Needs-driven
Characteristics	Funder decides what services farmers receive	Client pays for services; funder may support on temporary basis. Funder supports service providers and clients to build capacity and generate demand for services	Funders intervene where clients cannot pay for services by, for example, a combination of free-service provision and support to business service providers to make their services affordable. Funders' intervention is in agreement with farmers' needs and demands
Source of funds	Funder (government or donor)	Client, or subsidy from funder (to be phased out)	Clients pay if they can afford it. Funder pays for disadvantaged clients
Payment for services	Free for client	Client pays all or part. Vouchers for clients who cannot pay	Combination of free services, partly paid by clients, and fully paid by clients
Services offered	Decided by funder	Decided by funder on the basis of the believed potential market	Decided on the basis of clients' needs and existing demands
Delivery	Direct delivery by government or donor, or through contracted private-sector provider	Services provided by private sector	Services provided by private sector, public or NGOs, depending on their (local) comparative advantage
Inclusiveness	Can have wide coverage and reach poor and disadvantaged clients nationwide	Providers tend to serve better-off clients who can pay for services	Good: services are tailored for both subsistence and commercially-oriented clients
Accountability	Upward: providers accountable to funder. Clients have little say	Providers theoretically accountable to clients, but in practice often accountable to the funder supporting them	Downwards and upwards. Providers accountable to clients for fully paid services. Providers accountable to both farmers and funders for free or subsidized services. Providers' associations play important role in quality certification
Sustainability	Hard to maintain expensive services over time	Clients pay for services they demand; but providers often dependent on subsidies	For free or subsidized services, gradual phase-in of affordable prices for clients

paid services. It would require a mechanism of communication and coordination between different service providers, and a coherent donor support policy.

We can only start to work through such a concept here. This chapter provides some initial ideas on what such a system might look like.

A focus on needs

We can borrow some ideas from health care. In this field, as in agriculture, cost-effectiveness is important in deciding what services to provide. But it should certainly not be the only consideration. For example, a focus on cost-effectiveness alone may mean closing clinics in remote areas, depriving patients of vital treatment. Clearly, other criteria must also be taken into account to make sure that rural people also get the health care they need.

The word "need" here is key. A service (cosmetic surgery, say) may be very cost-effective but not needed, while another (malaria prevention) may be less cost-effective but be needed much more. Considering such needs is a way to prioritize such interventions (Østerdal et al. 2006).

Assessing needs

Different farmers have different needs, and outsiders' views of farmers' needs may be different from the farmers' own views. So how to design a system based on unclear needs? One way to do so is to look at what services smallholder farmers and other local value chain actors are looking for.

Services offered and which attract the attention of farmers or other value chain actors may be considered "needed". If farmers do not see the benefit of a particular service, they will not demand that it be provided, and they will not wholeheartedly buy into it.

That requires two additional pieces that are not given enough emphasis in the supply- and market-driven models: needs assessments and monitoring and evaluation.

- **Needs assessments.** Determining the farmers' needs is a vital first step. At first, this can be done through action-oriented studies of a particular subsector. Later on it can be incorporated into the policies and implementation plans of donors, national and local governments and associations of private-sector providers (see below).

- **Monitoring and evaluation.** Monitoring and evaluation systems are required that compare the demand for services with the supply, and that request feedback from clients on the quality of the services provided. The findings would then be incorporated into periodic adjustments in the service-delivery system.

Such systems could focus on a particular agricultural subsector (such as cereals), or on farming in a particular part of the country. Both types of focus have pros and cons.

Focusing on a **subsector** makes it easier to adjust the service provision to the requirements of enterprises concerned with that set of products. But this ignores the fact that most farmers raise many types of crops and livestock. The poor, women and disadvantaged may get missed out if, for example, the focus is on maize, which tends to be grown and sold by men who own bigger plots of land.

A focus on farming as a whole in a particular **geographical area** avoids these problems. It gives a better understanding of farmers' livelihoods and how service provision works. But it may have to cover too many crops and markets. That makes the design of service provision even more complex.

Public investment

For service providers to respond to different demands they require an environment that supports their activities. They also need different sources of funding. By themselves, private service providers will not address the needs of all farmers. Hence, targeted public investments in extension will remain crucial, even when services are delivered by non-state providers (GFRAS 2010). Public investment has two important roles: promoting an enabling environment, and directly supporting the provision of business services (by public, private or non-profit providers).

Promoting an enabling environment

Governments have an essential role in setting taxes and levies, providing mechanisms for business registration, and managing land and deed administration. They invest in roads, electricity and marketplaces. They govern the management of natural resources, particularly "the commons" such as forests, grazing lands and water bodies. Secure access to and sustainable management of these assets are important for many private-sector actors (Hilhorst et al. 2008).

In short, governments should make sure impediments to enterprise development are removed, and to establish conditions which encourage innovation. The precise role of government will vary from country to country. There is no single, unique role for government everywhere.

Supporting business service provision

A second major role for the public sector is to support the creation of pluralistic service markets. This does not mean a return to the supply-led model. On the contrary, in a needs-based model, this means the government becomes a regulator, facilitator and enabler.

A number of strategies for partial or full cost recovery have been discussed earlier in this book. They may need to coexist with fully government- or donor-paid services where there are market imperfections, infrastructure gaps or a food-security crisis.

It is no longer a question of how much public support or subsidy to provide. The challenge for governments is how best to design subsidies in a way that develops rather than distorts business markets.

Subsidizing back-up service providers is one way to go about this. This involves paying private companies or NGOs to support service providers to get set up, training them, expanding their businesses and overcoming their challenges. This approach has a number of big advantages when compared to supporting business providers directly:

- It does not distort the market for services, as the back-up providers do not compete in the same market.

- It provides a way to support capacity building and to improve the quality of local service provision, at much larger scale than if donors invest directly in service providers.

- It means that fewer costs have to be passed on to farmers for the services they get. The less they have to pay, the more services farmers can obtain.

- Working through back-up services makes it easier for governments and donors to coordinate their activities as they deal with fewer partners. It is the back-up providers who have an overview of the service provision supply and demand in a particular region or value chain.

- It provides an easy way for donors to withdraw: they can stop funding without compromising the direct provision of services to farmers.

Nevertheless, there is an implicit danger in this model of support. If the subsidized back-up service providers start providing services directly to farmers, they turn into unfair competition for the organizations they once trained and coached (CDASED 2001).

Principles of a needs-driven model

Based on the experience of the service providers described in this book, the following seem to be the principles of a needs-driven model:

- The public sector is committed politically and financially to a transition from disconnected supply-driven and market-driven interventions to a needs-based model.

- Services are seen as part of a larger system of actors within and outside the value chains, each of them with their own initiatives and interests.

- Various actors work in partnership to promote change. These actors include research, public and private extension, traders and processors, farmers and their organizations, NGOs, and local and national governments.

- Learning as a key element, both among such actors and between initiatives in different locations that face similar challenges.

The business of agricultural business services

- Government-funded extension systems are decentralized to the lowest possible level, accompanied by properly managed financial resources and mechanisms for public participation and monitoring. Extension services need to remain efficient and effective, while becoming more responsive to local needs and opportunities.

- NGOs, farmers' organizations and governments all work towards ensuring that farmers can clearly articulate their demand for services.

- Donors and governments subsidize back-up service providers. These provide training, coaching and general support to service providers to enable them to supply marketable services.

- Plural delivery channels exist, with private, public and non-governmental extension functioning side by side. This requires effective coordination of and collaboration among service providers.

- Delivery systems and monitoring and evaluation requirements make service providers accountable to their users.

- Staff of service providers (public, non-profit and private) can increase their skills and capabilities. Business services related competencies are incorporated into higher educational curricula. Mid-career professionals have opportunities to attend courses to upgrade their skills.

Further work is needed to understand how such a model would work out in practice.

Below are a number of recommendations for governments and donors, based on the experiences of the service providers who contributed to this book and the vision of a needs-driven model. These suggestions reflect what we consider an enabling environment for service providers working under a needs-driven model.

Recommendations to governments and donors

Agricultural extension policies

Governments need to recognize the value and importance of pluralism in business service provision, and to reflect this in their agricultural extension policies and strategies (Box 16). A funding commitment is needed, as well as room for the development of both private- and public-sector service providers.

It is also important to avoid local governments working against the private provider. Some services have important political implications – as with the land measurements done by the business service centres in Ghana. In such cases, good relations with the local government become vital.

Box 16   The African Union's Framework for Africa's Agricultural Productivity

African governments should support market-oriented agricultural extension. That is a recommendation from the African Union's Comprehensive African Agriculture Development Programme under the New Partnership for African Development (NEPAD).

This programme's Framework for Africa's Agricultural Productivity defines the main principles for market-oriented agricultural development in Africa. These principles translate into the following in particular (FARA 2006):

- **Service providers.** Extension services will increasingly be provided through performance-based contractual arrangements, rather than by civil servants. Potential extension service providers may include combinations of the private sector, NGOs, farmers' associations, universities, or any other entities with the capacity to provide extension services. In allowing for a plurality of providers, such arrangements take advantage of a broad array of already available field expertise.
- **Farmers' influence.** Farmers, through their groups and associations, will have significant influence over the allocation and use of agricultural services expenditures, e.g., by contracting extension service providers.
- **Covering costs.** The costs of extension are gradually shared with local governments, farmers' associations, and where possible with the producers themselves. For some commodities, such as cotton, sugar or poultry, agribusiness partners may support part of the cost of providing extension services.

Good working relations between the public and private service providers are important. Private providers have a clear role to play in attending to fully commercial farmers, but not only to them: they also have a potential role in serving subsistence farmers and those newly engaged with the market.

Coordination mechanisms

In a pluralistic extension system where public, non-profit and private-sector providers all serve farmers and other value chain actors, a mechanism for communication, coordination and division of tasks is needed. Here too, governments have a role to play. A policy framework is needed to define the agricultural extension strategy, demarcating geographical areas, farmer typologies, agricultural subsectors or types of services for combinations of private and public service provision and funding. For instance, agreements can be made indicating that the private sector delivers business services, while the local government invests in infrastructure or the provision of tangible items.

Such a policy could set up a private–public coordination body, which could set quality criteria and standards governing service quality in a region or sub-sector. This coordination body could also be responsible for liaising with donors and ensuring donors' understanding and buy-in into the overall extension strategy.

Back-up service providers can support the coordination between funders and service providers because they are familiar with the different initiatives in a certain area or value chain.

Don't crowd out the private sector

Government interventions in the sector need to be treated carefully. If not well-designed, free or subsidized services may end up crowding out private-sector providers. The playing field is often not level: public and NGO service providers are often tax-exempt, while private providers must pay.

In the same way, donors promote smallholder businesses as a way to alleviate rural poverty. Their investment often translates into grants to service providers and free services to clients. We have argued elsewhere in this book that such free services are important for a certain share of the rural population. But subsidies by donors, just like those by governments, can distort the emerging market for such services, and further tilt playing field away from private providers (Figure 66).

The indiscriminate provision of free services (both tangible items and business services) means farmers become used to getting things for free and averse of paying for services. An example of this is in Ghana, where the public services provide cocoa seedlings free of charge. In doing so, they are making life difficult for privately run nurseries which have sprung up to supply new hybrid varieties.

Any donor-funded programme therefore needs to consider which services are to be subsidized, how the private sector is to be involved, and what the exit strategy would be. Such a strategy could be based on the gradual recovery of service costs, or cost-effective ways of providing services, as described in the previous chapter under *Sustainability*.

Figure 66   If the playing field is uneven, private service providers can be left on the side-lines

This book has also described a number of ways to use public funding wisely to strengthen both the demand and supply side of service provision (see the earlier section on *Public investment*).

Design depends on context

The service provision depends on the context, so it is important to understand each situation. What services are already in place? Who currently provides the services, and how? To what extent do farmers supply local or external markets? What is the level of farmer organization? What do farmers need in terms of business development support? All these questions need to be asked during the design of donor- or government-led interventions.

A priority of donors and governments should be to support interventions which appear to offer a credible path to sustainability, i.e., which are finite and offer a realistic end to donor involvement. Interventions which do not offer a finite end for donor involvement or public funding need to be clear about their relevance and have a realistic strategy for long-term support.

The sustainability of interventions could be greatly enhanced by longer-term planning and a clear strategy for particular agricultural subsectors or geographical areas, as described in the previous section.

Tailor-made services

Services need to be tailored to the realities (and demand, or needs) of farmers. For some farmers, they will focus on (say) boosting crop yields rather than helping smallholders to reach markets. DLSP is an example of this: it provides food-security grants and agricultural advisory services to the poorest households; it offers enterprise grants and business-oriented advice to those who are shifting from subsistence to market-oriented agriculture.

As their production and income increase, farmers begin to demand new types of services. Initially, they may need technical advice to boost their production and product quality. Next, they may need help with organizational management and setting up a company or cooperative. Once such organizational issues have been tackled, the next step may be to link them to other value chain actors (buyers, processors, credit, other farmers). Excel Hort, for example, expects that when the farmer groups it is supporting are functioning well, the company will take on a brokering role, linking such groups to buyers.

As farmers become stronger economically, they also become better able to say what they want and need. And they are also more able to pay for the services they obtain.

Promoting the supply of pluralistic services

In practice, governments could do more to support the private sector, by supporting both supply of and demand for business services (Davis and Heemskerk 2012) – provided these business services tend to clients' needs. We look first at the supply.

Outsourcing. The government may outsource the provision of services to private companies or NGOs. This can be done, for example, by inviting service providers to bid for contracts to serve farmers in a particular area or in a particular value chain. Or the government could process requests by groups of farmers for support; the groups then choose their service provider. In doing so, it should take into account the comparative advantages of different service providers in different parts of the country, products or value chains.

Matching grants. Some donor-funded programmes have special matching-grant arrangements for private service providers. Aspiring service providers submit a business plan to the donor; successful applicants get a grant to cover a certain percentage of the start-up funds they need. They have to come up with the remainder of the funds themselves. This is common practice in IFAD- and World Bank-supported programmes, such as in Mozambique and Uganda (World Bank 2010, Heemskerk and Davis 2012).

Credit. Alternatively, donor-funded projects can provide a guarantee for banks, which in turn provide credit to service providers to establish their business. In Uganda, IFAD has found that the credit recipients often provide embedded services, which banks consider less risky than other models of business provision.

Research and development. The public sector may carry the burden of developing and testing new services through research, the public extension system or private back-up service providers. These services can later be implemented on a larger scale – and more cheaply – by different providers. See the *Sustainability* section in Chapter 7 for more.

Technical assistance and capacity building. Public money can also be used to support technical assistance for service providers and boost their capacity, for example through short courses, adapting university curricula, and coaching by back-up service providers.

Promoting social enterprises. Many private service providers operate as "social enterprises": they have two aims: making a profit, and improving farmers' livelihoods using commercial strategies. Public finance can be used to promote such an approach and make it easier for them to enter the market or to expand.

Stimulating demand for business services

Public investment can help organize and boost the demand for business services in various ways.

Organizing farmers. Organized farmers are better able to articulate their requirements, and it is easier to supply services to a group than to individuals. That reduces the cost per farmer and increases the potential client base and impact.

Information on services. The government can disseminate information on the types of services available and where farmers can get them. For this, an inventory of potential providers is needed. One way to develop such an inventory is for service providers to organize themselves into some kind of association or network.

Vouchers. Handing out vouchers can stimulate demand by encouraging reluctant clients to try a new service. This needs to be managed carefully, as experiences in this book confirm.

Service development and testing. This can trigger demand by exposing farmers and other value chain actors to a new service.

Quality assurance

As the service-provision market grows, the services have to meet appropriate standards. A system of registration or certification is needed to ensure they do so. Quality criteria need to be established, as well as operational guidelines for service providers and independent monitoring of their performance.

Registration in such a system should be voluntary to avoid threatening existing informal services (such as those provided by neighbouring farmers who are not registered as private companies and therefore do not pay taxes) and the emergence of innovative new providers. Registration and accreditation should be compulsory for service providers that apply for public-sector contracts.

The government might manage such a system, or the service providers themselves might do so through providers' associations.

Service providers' associations

Service providers could benefit from professional associations at the local, national or regional levels. An association, as piloted by 3C, could provide its members with information, an opportunity for exchange, mutual learning and professional development. It could provide a platform for quality control and advocating policy changes on, for example, taxation or educational curricula. It could also be used as springboard to reach educational institutes and engage in larger capacity building programmes.

Such associations could also provide a form of self-regulation and social responsibility. If clients complain, there should be a grievance system in which the complaint is checked and appropriate action is taken. Building up a civil society structure in this field and enhancing professional self-organization would merit support.

The African Forum for Agricultural Advisory Services (AFAAS, www.afaas-africa.org) is establishing country chapters of agricultural advisory service providers. These national forums include service providers, and education and training in business services and could play a catalytic role in bringing service providers together.

Reorienting agricultural education

The general need for qualified service providers in the public and private sector requires a reorientation of agricultural education. More business skills and knowledge should be included in the agricultural curriculum of universities and technical schools and colleges. Interactive training, with a balance between classroom training and practice, would train students to work in business service provision. Educational institutes can also play a role in coaching existing service providers – a role that back-up service providers such as Target Consultants and Miruku can also play.

Accountability to clients

The ways services are contracted can greatly enhance the accountability of extension to farmers. Governments and donors have an important role in demanding accountability, which can be part of the monitoring and evaluation efforts described under *Accountability* in Chapter 7. As illustrated by the cases in this book, service providers are too often accountable only to the donors, and not to their clients. Donor-funded projects need to monitor the performance of the service providers, with the direct involvement of the farmer clients.

One possibility, in theory, is to provide resources (such as vouchers) directly to farmers or their organizations so they can hire service providers. The problems with this model have been discussed elsewhere (see *Accountability*). Governments (in Mozambique and Malawi), international NGOs (e.g., Agriterra) and programmes (e.g., FAO) are experimenting with this option. Voucher models should be considered only after learning from these experiences.

An alternative is to give the final say to farmers' groups on which service provider to hire. The public Agricultural Technology and Agribusiness Advisory Services, in Uganda, are an example of this. In this case, service providers are chosen by and accountable to farmer forums. Under the national public extension programme in Mozambique, the responsibility for choosing and monitoring service providers lies with the district advisory councils, in which farmers' groups participate.

The public sector can also influence the quality of services that are provided privately. This can be done by creating and supporting associations or networks of local service providers, as described above.

Reaching the hard to reach

Donors and governments need to be proactive if their aim is to reach disadvantaged farmers. A proper needs assessment, services tailor-made for the target clients, and regular monitoring together with them are essential if this is to happen.

Most initiatives by both governments and international donors require smallholder farmers to get organized in groups and to work through associations, cooperatives and unions.

There are many good reasons for this. But groups are not a panacea: individual entrepreneurship is at least as important, also inside the groups. And working through groups does not guarantee the services will reach all the members: often, some farmers benefit more than others.

The business service system

Efforts to improve smallholder agriculture are often based on the idea that a limited dose of standardized outside help can stimulate farmers to achieve higher yields and incomes. "Help the farmers adopt an improved technology", goes the argument, "and get them organized and linked to a buyer, and they will be able to fend for themselves. They will no longer need outside help."

It is not that simple. As farmers get more productive and become more market-oriented, their capabilities increase, and their needs change. They start to require new types of services: advice on warehouse receipt systems rather than help with storing grain on the farm; crop insurance and assistance with drafting contracts rather than help with organizing a savings group. Their needs for services from outsiders do not fade away; they change. Providing such a wide range of services often surpasses what government and NGOs can do alone. At a certain point, they need to also rely on private-sector providers.

Some providers will remain generalists, offering a wide range of services; others will become specialists, focusing on a single type. They will collaborate on some aspects and compete on others. Farmers will shop around among competing providers to find the services they want. Governments and providers' associations will act as regulators and referees, making sure that the market for services is open and honest, and that certain groups are not disadvantaged. NGOs and public extension systems will fill in the gaps missed by the private sector. Innovation – new ways of doing things – will be tried by all, and quickly adapted to fit different realities.

Indeed, we might think of agricultural business services as a system. It depends on the way different organizations and individuals work – together or separated, is dynamic, and responds to changes in the environment.

But at the moment, reality is still far from this picture. Service providers tend to work in relative isolation. They compete with other service providers, so do not want to give away too much about their own business. They have contractual relationships with donors, who will monitor what they do, but not necessarily support them to learn from their mistakes and do things better. Relations with government are sometimes adversarial rather than collegial. And there are few training opportunities they can take advantage of.

One thing they do not lack is work. They have therefore little time to stop and reflect systematically on the work they do, and their contribution to society. Our intention in this book has been to give them the room to do so: to learn from each other and to reflect. We hope that we have succeeded in doing so, by generating lessons, suggesting how obstacles can be overcome, and triggering further questions from service providers, governments and donors alike.

References

Evaluating the performance of farmers' groups
Photo: Harun Thomas, FFARM, Ethiopia

References

Anderson, J.R. 2007. Background paper for the world development report 2008: Agricultural advisory services. World Bank, Washington, DC. http://tinyurl.com/ajhqggv

Belt, J., and W. Goris. 2011. Learning and earning: How a value chain learning alliance strengthens farmer entrepreneurship in Ethiopia. Bulletin 395. Royal Tropical Institute, Amsterdam, and Agri-ProFocus. http://tinyurl.com/asm8eab

Birner, R., K. Davis, J. Pender, E. Nkonya, P. Anandajayasekeram, J. Ekboir, M. Mbabu, D.J. Spielman, D. Horna, S. Benin, and M. Cohen. 2009. From best practice to best fit: a framework for designing and analyzing pluralistic agricultural advisory services worldwide. Journal of Agricultural Education and Extension 15(4): 341–55. http://tinyurl.com/ahuddkx

CDASED. 2001. Business development services for small enterprises: Guiding principles for donor intervention. Committee of Donor Agencies for Small Enterprise Development. World Bank, Washington, DC. http://tinyurl.com/bxg7j2g

Chipeta, S., I. Christoplos, and E. Katz. 2008. Common framework on market-oriented agricultural advisory services. Neuchâtel Group. http://tinyurl.com/bgkojdw

Christoplos, I. 2010. Mobilizing the potential of rural and agricultural extension. Food and Agriculture Organization of the United Nations and Global Forum for Rural Advisory Services. FAO, Rome.

Davis, K., and W. Heemskerk. 2012. Investment in extension and advisory services as part of agricultural innovation systems: An overview. AIS investment source book. http://tinyurl.com/b684yho

FARA. 2006. Framework for African Agricultural Productivity (FAAP). Forum for Agricultural Research in Africa, Accra.

GFRAS. 2010. Five key areas for mobilising the potential of rural advisory services. GFRAS Brief 1. Global Forum for Rural Advisory Services, Lindau, Switzerland.

Heemskerk, W., and K. Davis. 2012. Farming as a business and the need for local (agri-) business development services. In: AIS investment sourcebook. http://tinyurl.com/b4k65st

Hilhorst, T., G. Baltissen and E. Lodenstein. 2008. What can rural local governments contribute to private sector development? KIT Working Papers Series G2. Royal Tropical Institute, Amsterdam.

Kahan, D. 2007. Business services in support of farm enterprise development: A review of relevant experiences. Food and Agriculture Organization of the United Nations, Rome.

Kahan, D. 2011. Market-oriented advisory services in Asia: A review and lessons learned. Food and Agriculture Organization of the United Nations, Regional Office for Asia and the Pacific, Bangkok.

KIT, Agri-ProFocus and IIRR. 2012. Challenging chains to change: Gender equity in agricultural value chain development. KIT Publishers, Royal Tropical Institute, Amsterdam. http://tinyurl.com/bx-79jvq

Mundy, P., E. Mathias and I. Bekalo. 2006. Out of heads and onto paper. LEISA Magazine 22(1). www.mamud.com/Docs/outofheads.pdf

Østerdal, L.P., A. Hasmanii, and T. Hope. 2006. An inquiry into needs-based allocation of health care resources. www.econ.ku.dk/lpo/needs2.pdf

Osterwalder, A. 2004. The business model ontology: A proposition in a design science approach. Dissertation 173, University of Lausanne, Switzerland.

Osterwalder, A., Y. Pigneur and C.L. Tucci. 2005. Clarifying business models: Origins, present and future of the concept. Communications of the Association for Information Science 16: 1–25.

Spielman, D.J., J. Ekboir, and K. Davis. 2009. Developing the art and science of innovation systems enquiry: Alternative tools and methods, and applications to sub-Saharan African agriculture. In: Sang-inga, P. et al. (eds) Innovation Africa: Enriching farmers' livelihoods. Earthscan, London. Pp. 74–85.

Swanson, B.E., and R. Rajalahti. 2010. Strengthening agricultural extension and advisory systems. World Bank, Washington, DC.

UNDP. 2004. Business development services: How to guide. Bratislava Regional Centre, United Nations Development Programme.

Van Weperen, W. 2011. Market oriented agricultural advisory services: Guidelines for setting up MOAAS pilots. Study on market oriented agriculture advisory services (MOAAS) commissioned by Forum for Agricultural Research in Africa (FARA). www.kit.nl/smartsite.shtml?ch=KIT&id=72984

World Bank. 2007. World Development Report 2008: Agriculture for Development. World Bank, Washington.

World Bank. 2010. Designing and implementing agricultural innovation funds: Lessons from competitive research and matching grant projects. http://tinyurl.com/bjg2hlh

Contributors' profiles

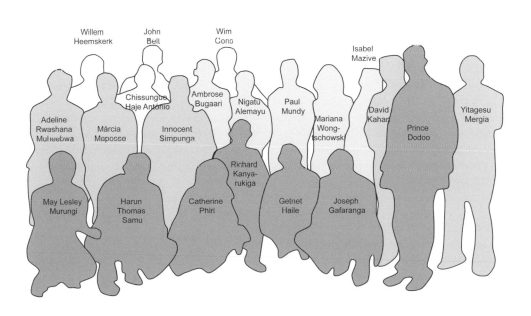

Willem Heemskerk

John Bell

Wim Gorio

Isabel Mazive

Adeline Rwashana Muheebwa

Chissungue Haje António

Ambrose Bugaari

Nigatu Alemayu

Paul Mundy

David Kahan

Yitagesu Mergia

Márcia Maposse

Innocent Simpunga

Mariana Wong-tschowski

Prince Dodoo

May Lesley Murungi

Harun Thomas Samu

Richard Kanya-rukiga

Catherine Phiri

Getnet Haile

Joseph Gafaranga

Contributors' profiles

Nigatu Alemayu
Research officer, Improving Productivity and Market Success of Ethiopian Farmers (IPMS)
Addis Ababa 5689, Ethiopia. Tel. +251 911897791, +251 6460259; email n.alemayehu@ cgiar.org, website www.ipms-ethiopia.org

Nigatu holds a BSc degree in agriculture from Alemaya College of Agriculture and an MSc in animal production from Alemaya University of Agriculture. He is currently studying for a PhD in environmental science at the University of South Africa. He has over 20 years of experience in development and research at the Ministry of Planning and Economic Development, and in the Ethiopian agricultural research system, the International Livestock Research Institute, private business and international NGOs. His current interests focus on commodity value chain development and business enterprise, technological and institutional innovations, and capacity building of public and private sector institutions in livestock, crops and horticultural commodities.

Chissungue Haje António
Executive director, Miruku
Mozambique. Tel. +258 824 541 310, 844 541 310, email haje.miruku@gmail.com, miruku@tdm.co.mz

Haje holds a master's degree in business administration from the Catholic University in Mozambique. He has 17 years of experience as a project manager, consultant in business development services, capacity building and training of trainers on setting up farmers' associations, business plan development for small and medium enterprises, organizational development and market linkages. He is an expert in result-oriented monitoring and business-oriented training modules sponsored by the International Labour Organization. He has practical experience on microfinance products for community projects and local economic development.

John Belt
Senior advisor, Royal Tropical Institute (KIT)
Mauritskade 63, 1092 AD Amsterdam, Netherlands. Tel. +31 20 568 8332, fax +31 20 568 8444, email j.belt@kit.nl, website www.kit.nl

John is an agricultural economist from Wageningen University with over 20 years of experience in rural development work in Africa, Asia and Latin America. He has lived in Colombia, Costa Rica, Mozambique, Yemen, Italy, Tanzania and Peru, working for and with research organizations, the United Nations, development NGOs and the private sector. He is currently senior economist at the Royal Tropical Institute (KIT), a knowledge institute on sustainable development based in Amsterdam. His expertise includes value chain development, private sector development, inclusive business, private–public partnerships, development finance and green economics.

Ambrose Bugaari

Consulting director and chief executive officer, Effective Skills Development Consultants (ESDC)
Kampala 24249, Uganda. Tel +256 752 573900, email ambrose_bugaari@yahoo.com, website www.esdconsults.com

Ambrose holds an MA in development studies and an MBA in management, both from Uganda Martyrs University-Nkozi. He also holds a BA degree in sociology and a postgraduate diploma in education Makerere University, Kampala. He specializes in agribusiness and conservation enterprises. He has 14 years of experience in enterprise development and rural livelihoods consulting, implementing donor-funded and international development programmes. Much of this work has been assisting rural communities in Uganda by providing technical skills and capacity building to help build sustainable businesses and improve livelihoods.

Prince Dodoo

Programme manager, Cocoa Livelihoods Program, Agribusiness Systems International (ASI)
B7/11 A&C Plaza, East Legon, Accra, Ghana. Tel. +233 27 7 788480, email niiamugi20@ yahoo.com, pdodoo@acdivocaghana.org

Prince is a Ghanaian development worker with a master's degree in agricultural economics from the University of Ghana, Legon. He specializes in project management, rural business service provision (especially in agricultural finance) and facilitation of linkages between key actors in commodity value chains, with a focus on farmers.

Joseph Gafaranga

Executive secretary, Urugaga Imbaraga–Northern Province, and President of Land Commission, Musanze district
PO Box 36, Musanze, Rwanda. Tel. +250 788 423 047, email gafarangajo@yahoo.fr

Joseph studied general agriculture and veterinary science at secondary level in Rwanda, and later pursued management studies in Bujumbura, Burundi. He has been in charge of day-to-day operations of Imbaraga–Northern Province for over 12 years. He has wide experience both as a participant and facilitator in the region and overseas, on issues of agricultural development, including human resources management, agricultural commodity value chains, marketing and entrepreneurship. He has played a significant role in shaping the current Rwandan land law, through which over 50% of farmers in Northern Province have acquired land titles. Himself a farmer, Joseph is a commercial grower of Irish potatoes, wheat and maize, and a friendly advisor to partners and colleagues.

Wim Goris
Network facilitator, Agri-ProFocus
PO Box 108, Arnhem, Netherlands. Tel +31 026 354 2056, email wgoris@agri-profocus.nl, website www.agri-profocus.nl

Wim was trained in tropical agriculture and worked in goat husbandry in northeastern Brazil. Later he joined Cordaid and worked on rural development and food security in Brazil and other countries in Latin America. As a network facilitator for Agri-ProFocus, his job is to get professionals from research, NGOs, and the public and private sectors working together around the demands of farmers and their organizations. His current portfolio includes "agri-hubs" (networks to promote entrepreneurship) in Ethiopia and Mozambique, and the theme "access to finance".

Getnet Haile
Manager, Target Business Consultants plc
PO Box 27619, Addis Ababa, Ethiopia. Tel. +251 911 211 989, 116 636 645, email getnet@ targetethiopia.com

Getnet is founder and manager of Target, a firm that provides consultancy services to businesses, NGOs and government offices in financial management, including training, financial manual development, and the computerization of accounting systems. Target has a portfolio of consultants in the agricultural, business and information technology professions. A chartered accountant with a master's in business administration, Getnet has attended short courses in consultancy services, business management systems and export marketing. He has conducted various studies on value chains, and helped develop organizational system and assessment of financial managements in Ethiopia, Djibouti, Uganda and South Sudan.

Willem Heemskerk
Senior advisor, Royal Tropical Institute (KIT)
Mauritskade 63, Amsterdam 1092 AD, Netherlands. Tel. +31 20 5688335, fax +31 20 5688444, email w.heemskerk@kit.nl, website www.kit.nl

Willem is a senior advisor on sustainable economic development and agricultural innovation. His expertise is in pluralist and multi-stakeholder agricultural research and advisory services, especially the role of farmers' organizations. He has more than 30 years of experience, 20 of which he has been based abroad. He has worked for various organizations in eastern, southern and western Africa, and has written numerous publications on demand-driven agricultural service delivery. His current focus is on sector policy, agricultural service delivery, capacity development and local governance, mainly in sub-Saharan Africa.

David Kahan
Senior officer, agricultural innovation and enterprise development, Food and Agriculture Organization of the United Nations (FAO)
Viale delle Terme di Caracalla, 00100 Roma, Italy. Email david.kahan@fao.org

David has a graduate degree in farm management extension and holds a PhD in agricultural management from the University of Reading, UK. He specializes in farm business management, enterprise development, marketing and agricultural extension, and developed the concept of the farm business school, which has been used in many countries in Africa. He has designed and supported a range of projects relating to services, value chain development and entrepreneurship development. He has also developed a range of training programmes and extension materials on related topics.

J. Richard N. Kanyarukiga
Senior lecturer, rural development and agribusiness, Higher Institute of Agriculture & Animal Production (ISAE)
PO Box 210, Musanze, or PO Box 3971, Kigali, Rwanda. Tel. +250 785 437 335, email jrnkanyarukiga@yahoo.com, jrnkanyarukiga@isae.ac.rw, website www.isae.ac.rw

Richard studied general agriculture and veterinary science in Tanzania, qualifying with a BSc in agriculture (animal science and production). Later, he studied tropical agricultural development, majoring in agricultural economics and planning at the University of Reading, UK, before pursuing his PhD in integrated water resources management at the University of Dar es Salaam, Tanzania. His research interests include agricultural policy analysis, marketing systems, commercialization and agricultural commodity value chain development, and gender equity. He has also served as director of research, community outreach and consultancy at ISAE. Apart from teaching and research, Richard is a consultant on socio-economic aspects of entrepreneurship, organizational development, and participatory development approaches. He co-manages Kf TRUST Agribusiness Ltd., a family firm engaged in poultry production, organic horticulture, training and consultancy.

Márcia Maposse
Production manager, Bindzu
Av. Ahmed Sekou Touré Nr. 1666 Maputo, Mozambique. Tel. +258 82 534 4639, email bindzu.agrobusiness@gmail.com, marciamaposse@hotmail.com

Márcia is Mozambican who holds a bachelor's degree in agricultural engineering from the Faculty of Agronomy and Forestry Engineering of Eduardo Mondlane University, Maputo. She specializes in agribusiness, and has extensive experience in field work and research, and in vegetable and sugarcane production in rural Mozambique.

Isabel Mazive
General manager, Dutch Agricultural Development & Trading Company (DADTCO)
Rua das flores, 2 andar Esquerdo, em frenteda ADEMO, Nampula, Mozambique. Tel +258 26 213 936, email i.mazive@dadtco.nl, website www.dadtco.nl

Isabel holds a graduate diploma in agriculture from Eduarmo Mondlane University in Maputo, and a master's in environmental management and development from the Australian National University. She has worked in the marketing department of the Mozambican Ministry on Industry and Trade, and for Biological Agriculture Biodiversity and Sustainable Development (ABIODES), a national NGO, as coordinator of the National Cotton Forum supportive project. She has experience in gender research, conservation farming, good agricultural practices, and the assessment of food availability and vulnerability.

Yitagesu Mergia
Freelance artist
PO Box 80280, Addis Ababa, Ethiopia. Tel. +251 911 485958, email yite_m@yahoo.com

Yitagesu is a freelance artist specializing in oil painting and graphic arts. He has an advanced diploma in fine art, and in 2009 graduated with a bachelor's in fine art and computer graphics from Addis Ababa University. He has also studied painting, sculpture, graphic arts and murals. He has drawn illustrations for publications and posters on gender, family planning, AIDS, agriculture and workers' rights. He specializes in using Adobe Photoshop to create artwork.

Adeline Rwashana Muheebwa
Agribusiness specialist, District Livelihoods Support Programme (DLSP)
PO Box 25770, Kampala, Uganda. Tel: +256 772 415 029, email ademuheebwa@gmail. com, website www.localgovt.co.ug

Adeline is a Ugandan consultant in agribusiness and development management. She holds an MSc and postgraduate diploma in development management from Milton Keynes University, UK, and a BSc in agricultural economics from Makerere University, Kampala. Her focus is on agribusiness, value chain analyses, gender and natural resources management. She has worked with various development agencies, including USAID, ILO, ASARECA and IFAD. She is a co-author of a book on environment, development and sustainability in the 21st century with the Open University, UK. She is currently working with District Livelihoods Support Programme under the Ministry of Local Government in Uganda, funded by IFAD. She is also the managing director of Humura Investments Limited a private firm that provides consultancy in value chain development and entrepreneurship in agriculture, gender and energy technologies.

Paul Mundy
Independent consultant in development communication
Müllenberg 5a, 51515 Kürten, Germany. Tel. +49 2268 801691, email paul@mamud.com, website www.mamud.com

Paul is a British consultant in development communication. He holds a PhD in journalism and mass communications from the University of Wisconsin-Madison. He specializes in easy-to-understand extension materials, developed through intensive writeshops like the one used to produce this book. He also provides consultancy services in various aspects of development communication. He has worked extensively in Africa, Southeast Asia, South Asia, Latin America and the Caribbean.

May Lesley Murungi
Programme manager, Excel Hort Consult Ltd
Mbarara, Uganda. Tel +256 774 885 272, 485 661 103, email maymurung@gmail.com, website www.excelhort.com

May is currently a programme manager at Excel Hort Consult Ltd in Uganda, an agribusiness and development company that seeks to improve livelihoods through value addition, land and water use management, natural resource utilization and conservation, and promoting food and income security through agroforestry, among others. She is a biologist with a background in education, and holds an MSc in biology (natural resources, ecology and conservation). Her interests include education and working with rural communities on value chain development, natural resource utilization and conservation as well as environmental change.

Catherine Phiri
Programme coordinator, 3C Development Management & Entrepreneurship Experts Ltd
PO Box 10101, Lusaka, Zambia. Tel. +260 21 1290185/97, 7800166, email cphiri.3c@gmail.com, kesejohnkwali@gmail.com

Catherine is currently completing her master of science degree in project management at Cavendish University in Lusaka. She holds a postgraduate diploma in monitoring and evaluation from Cavendish University, and an international diploma in project management from Cambridge University. Her specialization is in project management and coordination. She works part-time for 3C. (For more information about 3C, please contact Christian Chileshe, principal consultant, entrepreneurship development, 3C Development Management & Entrepreneurship Experts Ltd., cchileshe.3c@gmail.com.)

Harun Thomas Samu
Financial management advice officer, Facilitating Farmers' Access to Remunerative Markets (FFARM plc)
PO Box 10068, Addis Ababa, Ethiopia. Tel. +251 11 416 3522, 911 838134, email haron_thomas@yahoo.com, farm@ethionet.com

Harun is financial management advisor with a bachelor's in accounting and a minor in business management. He has also attended trainings in entrepreneurship and business planning with CEFE International, Germany, in financial management with Mango, UK, and cooperative management with the International Labour Organization. He has extensive experience throughout Ethiopia on capacity building and auditing of farmers' marketing organizations. He has prepared a manual on accounting systems for cereal banks, given training on accounting, and undertaken organizational diagnoses of cooperatives.

As one of the founders and senior staff in FFARM, he provides training in cooperative entrepreneurship and business plan development, advises on financial management, acts as an auditor and financial health check assessor, facilitates strategic plan development and organizational capacity diagnosis, and links marketing organizations to sources of finance.

Innocent Simpunga

Head of food security and sustainable agriculture, UGAMA CSC

PO Box 28, Gitarama, Rwanda. Email ugamacsc@rwanda1.com

Innocent Simpunga holds an MSc degree in tropical and international agriculture from the University of Göttingen in Germany, and an MSc degree in crop sciences from Wageningen University in the Netherlands. He also has BSc degrees in soil sciences from ISAE Busogo, Rwanda, and in population studies from Université Libre de Kigali in Rwanda. He has done research on rice and potatoes in Rwanda, and has participated in local, regional and international conferences and workshops on irrigation development, vegetables, cassava and potato seed production. Innocent has a broad experience in entrepreneurship, organizational development, participatory development approaches, value chain development and consultancy services. Besides his work with UGAMA CSC, he is also visiting lecturer at the Catholic Institute of Kabgayi, Rwanda, on various aspects of agriculture, organization and management. He does research, community outreach and consultancies with several local and international NGOs.

Mariana Wongtschowski

Senior advisor, local economic development, Royal Tropical Institute (KIT)

Mauritskade 63, 1092 AD Amsterdam, Netherlands. Tel. +3120 5 688 481, email m.wongtschowski@kit.nl, website www.kit.nl

Mariana is a Brazilian agronomist with an MSc in agricultural knowledge systems from Wageningen University, Netherlands. In 2003 and 2005, she worked as a policy officer for the Dutch Ministry of Foreign Affairs, where she managed and supervised several projects on agriculture and natural resources management and agriculture, biodiversity and indigenous peoples. Until 2011, she worked with the ETC foundation, a Dutch-based non-governmental organization, where she was involved in and managed several programmes. One of them, Farmer Access to Innovation Resources, focused on piloting local innovation support funds in eight countries in Africa and Asia, facilitating learning among the countries and the projects' many partners. In her current position at KIT, she focuses on agricultural innovation and market-oriented advisory services.